ASTRO

Gregory Szanto practised for fourteen years first as a barrister and then as a solicitor before becoming involved in astrology. He resumed his studies at the Faculty of Astrological Studies where he obtained his diploma. He is now a tutor at the Faculty and has also served on its Council. He is a full-time consultant astrologer and founder of the Institute of Astrotherapy. He is married and has two children.

GREGORY SZANTO

ASTROTHERAPY
ASTROLOGY AND
THE REALIZATION
OF THE SELF

A NOVEL

ARKANA

LONDON AND NEW YORK

First published in 1987 by Arkana
(Routledge & Kegan Paul Ltd)
11 New Fetter Lane, London EC4P 4EE

Published in the USA by
Routledge & Kegan Paul Inc.
in association with Methuen Inc.
29 West 35th Street, New York, NY 10001

Set in Bembo 10/11½pt.
by Witwell Ltd, Liverpool
and printed in Great Britain
by The Guernsey Press Co Ltd
Guernsey, Channel Islands

Library of Congress Cataloging in Publication Data

Szanto, Gregory, 1944–
Astrotherapy: astrology and the realization of the
self.

Bibliography: p.
Includes index.
1. Astrology and psychotherapy. I. Title.
BF1729.P83S97 1987 133.5'815 86–32251

British Library CIP Data also available
ISBN 1-85063-059-3

I dedicate this book to
my family,
and to a few mad Hungarians

In the very depths of this formless mass you have implanted – and this I am sure of, for I sense it – a desire, irresistible, hallowing, which makes us cry out, believer and unbeliever alike: 'Lord, make us *one*.'

Teilhard de Chardin *Hymn of the Universe*

Contents

Illustrations

Acknowledgements

I acknowledge with grateful thanks those of my clients who have so generously and courageously agreed to their Birth Charts being used to illustrate the ideas in this book and especially Alicia, Rosalind, Christine and Pauline.

I should also like to thank my wife for her unfailing support and her love in providing a living example of harmony which enabled this book to be written.

Gregory Szanto
1986

CHAPTER 1
What is Astrotherapy?

1 *The healing of the nations – the union of Astrology and Psychotherapy*

We moderns are faced with the necessity of rediscovering the
life of the spirit; we must experience it anew for ourselves.

CARL JUNG[1]

Never before has the human race been filled with such promise as
we approach the end of the twentieth century. And yet never
before has the threat that faces mankind been so great as the next
millennium draws nearer. Man has become alienated from his
source and from the universe of which he is a part. The divisions
that exist in the world today reflect the disharmony within the
human psyche. If mankind is to fulfil its promise for the future it is
essential that these divisions, without and within, are healed.

I believe that we can bring about the healing of the human
psyche, which in turn will bring about the healing of the nations,
by uniting the insight which is contained in the ancient art of
astrology with the knowledge gained in the modern science of
psychotherapy. For the aims of both are the same. Each in its own
way seeks to put the individual in touch with his real self, with
what Jung has called the 'spirit'. It is therefore no coincidence that
the birth of psychoanalysis as the precursor of psychotherapy took
place at the same time as the resurgence of astrology.

Astrology has always recognized that the human psyche and the
universe are one and the same, and that the one is but a reflection
of the other. The Horoscope is both the symbolic representation
of the human psyche and the universe at the moment the
individual is born. It follows that if the individual is at one with

1

himself the universe will reflect his inner harmony. The goal of psychotherapy is to bring about this harmony within the psyche by enabling the individual to experience himself as a whole and so balance the conflicting aspects of his nature. The goal of astrology when used as therapy is to provide the means to see the psyche as a whole so that the individual can experience his true nature and transform the conflicts within him.

Astrology's potential as therapy has so far remained unrecognized. The intuitive realization of the nature of the human psyche possessed by our ancestors has been eroded with the gradual development of consciousness and rational analysis. And in the process the real meaning of astrology has been lost. I sought to describe that meaning in *The Philosophy of Astrology*[2] so that astrology can once again bring about a greater understanding of man's place in the universe. My purpose in writing this book is to show how astrology can be used specifically in terms of the understanding and healing of the human psyche so that the new discipline which I have called Astrotherapy can provide mankind with the means of rediscovering its spirit in this age.

Strictly speaking psychology is concerned with the understanding of the human psyche, while psychotherapy is concerned with the healing of the psyche. In reality the two are aspects of one integral process. The process of therapy, or healing, is the process of making whole, for it is when the divisions that exist in the psyche are united that the individual finds his spirit. The problem that the therapist faces is that he is unable to see the individual as a whole because he lacks a model of the individual psyche.

Astrology is unique in that in the Horoscope it alone possesses a model of each individual human psyche. Provided that this model is perceived in the right way it can afford a view of the spirit that is within each one of us. The problem that the astrologer faces is that in analysing the Horoscope he destroys the total, unique pattern which is never repeated and loses sight of the spirit. Thus, instead of healing the divisions within the individual, he enforces them.

The problem of being able to see the whole, and thus of being united with our spiritual nature, is a real one both in astrology and therapy which needs to be faced at the outset. Because we, on the material level, are divided, we inevitably see the parts. We see the separate aspects of the psyche and the constituent elements in the Horoscope. In itself it is perfectly valid to see the parts, but the danger is that we can get attached to them and fail to see that they lead to a greater whole. In traditional astrology, by assigning fixed meanings to the separate factors in a Birth Chart, we are left with no more than a list of empty character traits. Instead of finding the meaning of the individual's life, we discover only how he functions.

The same danger is often to be found among therapists. Anthony Storr, for example, having stressed the need for integration or union of the psyche, goes on to complain that '... we have as yet no reliable yardstick of innate human differences, no knowledge which would help us to predict and make provision for the differing requirements of different temperamental endowments.'[3] Anyone familiar with the Horoscope would point out that here is contained in a clear visual model the very thing that Storr is seeking. But having these separate characteristics, while useful as a means of personality assessment, is of no use whatever in seeing a person as a whole and discovering who he is as an individual.

Thus we inevitably see the parts. The therapist sees his patient's complexes projected onto the world outside; the astrologer sees the Sun in Taurus square Saturn. What matters, however, is what we see when we look at these parts. Astrology is a symbolic system and the reason why it is now poised to lead mankind into the new consciousness of the future is that we are finally coming to the realization, scientists as well as artists, that reality is symbolic. The material world, as well as the human psyche and the Horoscope, is a symbol. This means that we see not only the outer form – but the inner meaning through that outer form. The planetary bodies in themselves, in their mundane aspect, are material and they exist on the physical level just as the universe and each one of us exists on a physical level. Yet within this level, not as a separate part of it, but as its essence, is contained a spiritual level. And symbolism means perceiving the spiritual level in the outer, physical form – and in recognizing that the one is contained in the other.

Transformation, which is the ultimate goal of therapy and which involves becoming the people we are, can only be attained once the essence, the inner meaning, has been reached. It is therefore the ability to see this inner meaning that the astrologer must learn in order to use his art as therapy. This involves two things. First, it means seeing the Horoscope as the model of the individual psyche *as a whole*. And second, it implies seeing the inner meaning, or the spirit, in each separate factor as well as in the whole.

Astrology is ultimately a way of seeing and it is this astrological perception that will, I believe, enable mankind to discover its spiritual nature. Let us look at the Horoscope illustrated in Figure 1.1. That is a symbol of an individual human psyche. It is a whole pattern just as the psyche is a living organism, a total complex process, unique and entire in itself, which together makes up that individual and no other. Each separate part of this pattern forms a subtle relationship with every other part. It is only when this person becomes whole that she can find her real self, that she can find out who *she* is, and that she can find her inner being which is her spirit.

The way to see as a whole, and the way to enable the individual to experience his wholeness which is the healing process, is what I shall describe in this book. How then can we attain this unity of perception? There are three stages to this goal. First, we shall see the energies that are contained in the individual psyche in their ideal state of perfect balance when we look in chapter 3 at the model of the Tree of Life in the system of the Kabbalah. Psychotherapy not only lacks a model of the individual psyche but it has no single accepted model of the ideal psyche. By looking at the same energies that are found in the Horoscope on the Tree, we

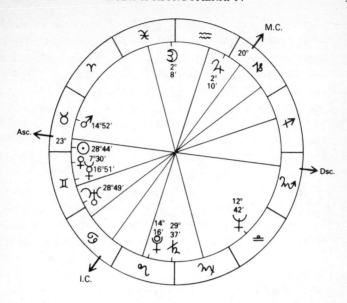

Figure 1.1 *Horoscope of Rosalind*

can see the ideal goal towards which each individual aspires, and thus come to a deeper understanding of the particular in the context of the universal.

Second, in chapters 4 and 5, we shall see that each separate factor in the Horoscope is itself a whole. Thus, each part contains its own integral continuum in time and space and in the same factor can be seen the past, the present and the future. Traditional astrology tends to isolate rather than integrate the meaning of the factors whereas in reality each factor in itself contains the means of its own transformation. Furthermore, if we look at the factors in what I have elsewhere called the fifth dimension, we can see that each factor is not only connected to, but is derived from, the other factors in the Horoscope. Thus multiplicity proceeds from unity and the process of healing can be regarded as a return to the original source.

Third, in chapters 7 and 8, we shall see the separate factors in the context of the Horoscope as a whole. Here too, traditional astrology, by assigning fixed meanings to the separate parts, fails to reconcile those parts into a whole. If we take the factors in isolation, and I include in the term 'isolation' the Sign, House and aspects, we are no nearer the real meaning of the individual psyche.

The question that each one of us in his own way asks is: 'Who am I?' It is the task of the therapist to help the individual to answer this question so that he is in touch with his true self. That true self is reflected in the pattern in the heavens at the moment of our birth. The task of the astrologer, then, is to enable the individual to perceive his unique pattern so that he can experience it and be at one with himself. If we can in this way change our perception of ourselves so that we see our spiritual nature and the meaning of our lives, then we shall change our perception of the world itself to reflect the harmony within ourselves.

2 *These earthly godfathers – the historical perspective*

> These earthly godfathers of Heaven's lights
> That give a name to every fixed star,
> Have no more profit of their shining nights
> Than those that walk and wit not what they are.
>
> William Shakespeare *Love's Labours Lost*

Let us at this point look to see why astrology has once again come into prominence after its long period of relative neglect. I believe that astrology has become stuck in the past and at present it is going through a transitional period of flux and uncertainty. If it is to emerge from this stage and meet the needs that brought about its resurgence, then it is necessary for us to be aware of those needs. This is particularly important if we are to appreciate why astrology has not yet been accepted so far by the younger sciences of psychology and psychotherapy.

I began this chapter with a quotation from Jung who stated that the greatest need for mankind today is to find again the life of the spirit. And I stated in the previous section what I believe this 'life of the spirit' to be. I did this because there are two separate aspects of the 'spirit' and in one is highlighted the division that exists between therapists today. In the general sense of realizing one's essence, of being in touch with one's centre or wholeness, the goal implied in this term is generally accepted.

Jung, however, in using the term 'spirit', places the emphasis on the inner life, on meaning or self-fulfilment, as opposed to the solution of practical problems, and in particular dealing with relationships that are emphasized by more traditional therapists. As we shall see in the next chapter when we examine the many different schools that exist in psychotherapy today, the divergence in viewpoint is a very real one.

The divergence in itself is valid enough for it reflects the split between the active and the receptive sides of the human psyche. That is why I have sought to stress that, in using the term 'spirit', I am concerned with the individual's essence which is only to be found in the union of both sides of the psyche. The very fact that each person is an individual implies that each person's needs will lie more in one direction than another, and also that each person will find one type of therapy more suited to his particular needs.

So it is that each age will emphasize one side more than the other, and while for many the practical problems of the world are as pressing as they have always been, nonetheless if we look at this age in perspective it should be clear that the search for a more general, inner fulfilment, a search for the 'spirit' in the specific sense that Jung has used the term, is a peculiar phenomenon of our times, and also that it is likely to be the most immediate need for those who are attracted to astrology as a means of healing.

If we go back to the origins of astrology we find that this split did not exist, for the spiritual and the material aspects of life reflected each other. For the ancients the mundane occurrences of the world were the manifestations of a divine will. The Emperor in China embodied the qualities of heaven. Our ancestors were as concerned with practical matters as we are today but they did not separate these concerns from their spiritual nature. Man, in ancient times, sought meaning as he seeks meaning today. But the nature of this meaning differed according to his view of the universe.

Then man lived in an uncertain world. He was threatened by a nature that appeared as a hostile force. He lived in a world where floods, fire, lightning could destroy his crops, his home and his livelihood. In those conditions, when material uncertainty was rife, meaning was synonymous with security and order. In seeking this order in an ever-changing world, he saw that in the heavenly bodies alone there existed a pattern which was repeated constantly in its unceasing cycles. In spite of the terror by night, and the destruction by day, with each dawn the sun rose upon his world and renewed its promise.

And because there was at that time no split between his body and his spirit, or between his conscious and unconscious nature, he saw in the order of the heavenly bodies a reflection of the divinity whose spirit infused his world. Here, in the perpetual cycles of the planets, in the daily rising of the sun and the never ceasing fluctuations of the moon, he saw the principles of eternity, the manifestation of a divine power that pervaded his life and that had existed before time and that would continue until time itself ceased to be.

It was therefore inevitable that once the divine order was replaced by material security and intellectual certainty, the needs that astrology had originally been developed to meet ceased to be effective. Periods of such relative order have alternated with times of relative chaos throughout history, when men turned now towards and now away from the astrologers and cunning men who have always existed in various guises in society.

When security finally permeated the material order as never before in the seventeenth century, astrology and its twin sister magic fell into desuetude. The political disorder that had culminated in the Civil War eventually ended with the restoration of the monarchy in 1660. The mysteries of the universe were explained by the new science of Newton and his colleagues who demonstrated that the planets were merely physical bodies that obeyed the same inexorable laws as all other inanimate objects. And the material danger of losing one's home and possessions by the sudden and ever-threatening risk of fire or loss at sea was largely obviated with the advent of insurance.

Since that time the security that men had sought in the heavens was increasingly to be found in the world around them. And this material security was matched by a greater intellectual certainty. The rational explanation that burgeoned with Newton left little scope for metaphysical speculation. Ever since then the sense of material order and rational understanding that mankind has enjoyed has steadily increased, at least for those fortunate enough to live in the 'civilized' world.

At the same time the explanation that science provided excluded spiritual belief. Without the heavens to provide a reflection for man's spiritual needs, the spirit was forced to dwell in places built by man himself – and thus became embodied in the state and political doctrines which were themselves but a reflection of man's materialism, or alternatively in the authority of an increasingly sterile form of orthodox religion whose spiritual centre had long since disappeared.

In this climate, with no place for the spirit to reside in the outside world, people were forced to look inside their own minds to find the divinity that no longer existed outside. So the science of psychology, and later psychotherapy, was born. So too, to answer the same needs, did people turn to the ever-growing 'alternative' disciplines and beliefs that flourish today – to yoga, meditation, eastern religions, the occult and esoteric arts, and, of course, to astrology.

This gradual search for meaning, the quest for a spiritual dimension to life, arose, then, to fill the existential void, the sense of alienation from his source, that mankind has progressively felt in his over-materialistic world. Then, in addition to the spiritual vacuum, the material order too began to crumble from the beginning of this century. In science, since the quantum revolution, the fixed, determinate laws of Newton are no longer accepted. Ecologically, the fine balance which is necessary for the survival of life on earth is in danger of being destroyed through pollution and the erosion of large areas of our planet. Socially, the family structure is breaking down and millions have lost, not only the opportunity of finding fulfilment through work, but even of earning a living. And perhaps most awesome of all, is the peril of nuclear war that threatens to obliterate the major part of human life as we know it.

Mankind today as never before needs to find meaning. His very survival depends upon his success. He needs to find his spirit. But the vital point which I believe must be stressed, if astrology is to meet its potential as a form of therapy, is that the spirit must be found in this world of ours and not by trying to escape from it. What has happened in the past is that the spirit has become separated from the world and from our lives. The temptation then is to seek this 'spirit' outside ourselves, and the real danger that must be faced is that in seeking meaning through alternative ideas people avoid real meaning, instead of filling the world with the true spirit which alone can make this world a better place. The real imperative for this new age is for the spiritual and material aspects of life to be united again. This is what wholeness and the healing process means.

We need astrology today, as a form of therapy, in order to bring back the union of the material and the spiritual that was inherent in its original philosophy and that reflected the unity of its origins. This is the true potential of astrology if it is to meet the needs of mankind for the future. Science and religion were once united in astrology. In separating the two man's psyche has become divided and union cannot be achieved in either direction alone.

Astrologers, as philosophers and representatives of the great occult traditions of the world, have always been concerned as much with practical as with spiritual matters, for each is but one aspect of the same principle. The spirit can be found anywhere. It is our centre. The way we arrive there is the personal question that each of us is asked in this incarnation. The way we answer that question provides the role of the new science of Astrotherapy that we shall now explore.

3 *A pure river – the role of astrology as therapy*

And he showed me a pure river of water of life, clear as crystal, proceeding out of the throne of God and of the Lamb.

In the midst of the street of it, and on either side of the river, was there the tree of life, which bare twelve manner of fruits, and yielded her fruit every month: and the leaves of the tree were for the healing of the nations.

Revelations 22:1

How then can astrology be used as therapy? Let me begin by making it quite clear what I mean by therapy and just what it is that I believe the astrologer can do in this respect. I am not of course suggesting that astrologers should, without proper training, set up to heal the mentally sick. In chapter 2 I shall look briefly at the state of psychotherapy today. Lest anyone, however, should fall into the trap of believing that psychotherapy is a clearly defined subject, let me just quote the opening words of the author of *What is Psychotherapy?* where he describes his initial experience of psychotherapy: 'No one could define it, controversy raged over the question of its effectiveness, different schools engaged in constant warfare with one another, and the training programme itself lacked goals and a coherent structure.'[4]

This is perhaps, to some extent at least, inevitable, for psychotherapy has many aims and many different people are involved in its work. Some are fully trained psychiatrists who deal with the mentally sick. At the other extreme there are counsellors, those engaged in social work, priests and welfare workers who have undergone a minimum of training and are concerned with more specific ends. It may of course be objected that there is a difference between therapy and counselling, for the former should involve treatment in the sense of healing while the latter should incorporate advice. Nevertheless, one does not always find this distinction made in practice, and this in itself naturally increases the controversy concerning the nature of psychotherapy.

Having made the general point that there is no agreement on virtually any of the fundamental bases of the subject, it is still possible to find a general aim among psychotherapists. In some way the therapist seeks to enable his patient, or client, to get in touch with his real self. The patient has problems which are either specific or general. He may be suffering from schizophrenia, he may be unable to cope with his marriage, he may lack a sense of purpose in life. Naturally the approach to each of these problems will be very different and their treatment will demand very different skills. Nevertheless the underlying aim, deliberately simplified, of both those therapists who seek to heal the sick mind and those who aim to provide understanding for people who are not clinically sick, is the unity or integration of the psyche.

In some way, therefore, the therapist tries to get the individual to realize his true self. He needs to face, and experience the nature of, his conflicts which lie within his unconscious. As I have pointed out, the problem that the therapist faces is that he cannot see the individual as a whole, and specifically he cannot see what lies in his unconscious. In order to bring out the elements of the unconscious the therapist needs something which will reflect that dark side. This reflection is achieved through the relationship between himself and the patient. Thus by a process of projection and transference the patient gradually comes to experience himself in his entirety. However, this reflection can easily become distorted because the therapist will himself project his own nature and conflicts onto the patient. The waters become muddied and the therapist needs to ensure that he can see the patient as he really is through his own counter-transferences and projections. It is for this reason that those like Anthony Storr have sought an objective way of seeing the individual psyche.

It is here that astrology can provide the ideal complement to psychotherapy. For the Horoscope is the reflection of the individual in his wholeness. All that is within the individual, conscious and unconscious, is contained in the wheel of the Birth Chart. The vital proviso is that the Horoscope is seen in the right way. The dilemma can be stated in this way. The need is for the individual to experience himself as a whole in order to heal the divisions within himself so that he can find out who *he* is and discover his own spirit.

In order to bring about this personal experience a relationship needs to be effected so that the individual can see those aspects of his psyche which are hidden. To use astrology as therapy the symbolism of the Horoscope needs to be used specifically in the process of therapy. Just as the therapist forms a relationship between himself and the patient so that the patient can see his own self reflected in the therapist, so the astrologer needs to effect a relationship for the spirit that is contained in the Horoscope to be reflected.

This involves the creation of a relationship between the client and his Horoscope and also between the client and the astrotherapist. In this way, and in this way alone, can the Horoscope be used in therapy to draw out the reality of the individual. And in this way a third force is brought into existence which unites the client, the Horoscope and the astrotherapist. So the Horoscope becomes the 'Thou' to the client's 'I'. Instead of being a two-dimensional model which is used only as a means of analysis, it becomes the living myth that contains the individual's being, the meaning of his life.

Although an increasing number of astrologers are now practising some form of psychotherapy the two disciplines have remained separate. The reason for this situation lies in the fact that, although both astrologers and therapists talk of wholeness, in practice they break down the essential integrity of the psyche and of the Horoscope which reflects it. Those astrologers who are involved in therapy use the Horoscope, if at all, only as a means of preliminary diagnosis and then proceed to the practice of therapy independently. Thus the real potential of astrology as a means of experiencing the individual's true self is not fulfilled.

To use astrology as therapy one needs to follow two steps. The first is to learn to perceive the Horoscope as the reflection of the individual psyche as a whole. If we look at Figure 1.1 we can see a lady with a number of separate characteristics symbolized by the various factors in her Horoscope. We can see her Moon in Pisces opposite Saturn, her Mars in the 12th House square Pluto, her Venus in Gemini. If we analyse these separate factors we can see her conflicts and we can also see her potentials. If, however, we also see those factors as parts of a whole, we can help her to become whole, we can enable her to realize her true self and get in touch with her spirit. Then she can begin to work through her conflicts and transform them and then the process of therapy is brought into being.

The second step, which consists of the experience of one's self as a whole, then flows from the initial prerequisite of perceiving the psyche as a whole. Although natal astrology can be used simply to understand a human being from an abstract point of view, once the client is introduced and the astrologer seeks to help him to understand himself, he is automatically moving towards therapy. How far he pursues the goal of therapy in practice will naturally depend on his training. It goes without saying that the untrained astrologer will be no better qualified to deal with psychiatric disorders than the marriage counsellor. But psycho-therapy as a discipline has been expanding its scope even within the lifetime of Freud. That scope is now poised to embrace the unity of perception which astrology alone is able to supply.

To provide a living relationship between the individual and his Horoscope whereby that individual is enabled to experience the reality of himself in his wholeness is, I believe, the real promise that astrology holds for the future. Then astrology can use the understanding of the psyche that psychotherapy has developed and the two can provide a living synthesis for the benefit of mankind and the healing of the nations.

CHAPTER 2
Psychotherapy

1 *The state of psychotherapy today*

Not all psychotherapists today would agree with the opinion of Jung that I quoted at the beginning of chapter 1. Indeed few psychotherapists today would agree with each other's views. Although I have answered the most fundamental question: 'What is psychotherapy?' in the last chapter by stating that it is the means of healing the human psyche, once we get beyond that basic acceptance, we find considerable confusion.

Of theory there is no shortage. There are now well over a hundred schools and the number is increasing steadily. While this is a healthy sign of a dynamic, developing discipline, it inevitably adds to the confusion. The fact that we find no consistent answers to the basic questions does not, in my view, matter. Psychotherapy has now developed far beyond its original horizons and embraces a wide variety of practitioners who work towards many different goals to meet the needs of an increasingly diverse body of patients and clients.

What, I believe, is important, is that we should be aware of these different aims and needs and resist the temptation to be dogmatic in insisting that one view alone is valid. It is inevitable, and natural, for astrologers, and those attracted to astrology, to find certain schools of therapy more congenial than others, but it is also important that astrology should develop in the context of psychotherapy as a whole.

In order to achieve this end we need to be aware of the current state that exists in this fascinating subject, and in this chapter I shall give a brief survey of the situation today. In doing so it will be necessary to keep the subject in perspective. As new discoveries and insights are made in any developing discipline, there can be a tendency to jettison too readily the old knowledge and embrace only the new. In doing so, one can end up without the foundations that are contained in the original discoveries. This is as true of astrology where we see some theorists employing techniques like harmonics and mid-points to the exclusion of traditional astrology, of science where the discoveries of Einstein and quantum physicists were built upon the shoulders of the old science. In therapy, too, there is the tendecy to associate only with Jung or some of the modern alternative schools, with Maslow or Assagioli, to the exclusion of Freud and his followers. We should of course be aware, and learn from the moderns, but we should also bear in mind that these new theories have been built on the shoulders of the pioneers and do not replace or invalidate their ancestors. Jung himself regarded his approach as empirical and warned against those who were so attracted by the gaudy feathers of new theories that they would do anything to avoid facing themselves.

If we are to use psychotherapy, and combine it with astrology in order to help our fellow men and women, then we must face ourselves – openly and honestly. And in doing so we should constantly bear in mind that every practising therapist, of whatever persuasion he may be, is trying in his own way to heal an individual's psyche and thereby to enable him to live, in his own way, a more fulfilling life. How he does this naturally depends to a great extent on his own temperament and on the needs of that individual patient or client, and in most cases the two will hopefully coincide.

It is not a question of which therapy is right and which is wrong. Nor is it a question of which therapy corresponds best to the Birth Chart. Astrology, as I will show in the course of this book, is its own therapy. We need, in looking at the development and current state of psychotherapy, to see how the different schools achieve their basic aims, what they have in common, in reality if not in terminology, and how they genuinely differ both in their aims and in their techniques. Then we can, to paraphrase Jung: learn the best, know the best – and forget everything when we face the Horoscope.

What I shall concentrate on therefore in surveying the situation in psychotherapy today is first, the similarities that exist beneath the confusion on the surface, and second, the genuine differences in approach that are present. In taking this approach I shall inevitably deal more fully with the early development of the subject rather than with the diversity of alternative schools that have proliferated in recent times. This is not to devalue the genuine importance of the latter but rather to stress the foundations and the fundamental principles that exist beneath the surface. For at the end of the day there is only one psyche, reflected in one Birth Chart. To get in touch with that psyche through its reflected Horoscope we must begin, like Perceval, by asking the right question.

Let us then look at some of the basic questions and see if we can find answers to them. Having answered the first question: 'What is psychotherapy?' by saying that it is the means to heal the psyche, we find that even at this stage we are not free from difficulties. What does healing mean? Once again, I have answered this in the literal sense of making whole and so of enabling the individual to be in touch with the whole of himself or herself and this too as a basic goal is largely accepted in principle, if not perhaps in practice. But at this point we find the first important divergence in the development of psychotherapy which still divides practitioners.

The founder of psychoanalysis, and thus of the whole psychotherapeutic movement, was Sigmund Freud. As a medical practitioner, he was naturally concerned with healing in the physical sense, and his original interest of what was to become the science of the mind arose as he came to recognize the connection between physical health and mental functioning. Thus, in its original form, the discipline had as its aim that of enabling people to become healthy individuals through the understanding of their minds. However, since its inception, both psychotherapy in general, and Freud's own ideas in particular, were to develop to the extent that the subject was no longer regarded as an adjunct of medical science and the emphasis came to be on the understanding of the human mind in its own right as much as on healing in the medical sense.

This divergence of approach has continued, and indeed has become more sharply defined, to this day. Many practitioners today adhere so strictly to Freud's original ideas that they have refused to accept his own later development. For these psychotherapy is still strictly a branch of the medical profession and it is thus virtually synonymous with psychiatry. The conflict came to a head in Freud's own lifetime when he argued strongly that psychotherapy was a branch of psychology rather than medicine and that therapy should be practised by laymen as well as doctors.[1] Today the former view is held chiefly in the USA where the body of psychoanalysts are almost wholly made up of medical practitioners and the latter in Europe where lay analysts are recognized in the profession.

The disparity between these viewpoints, and their consequent practice, opens up related questions as to the purpose of psychotherapy and the nature of its recipients as much as the more closely related question concerning its practitioners. For better or worse, psychotherapy is not now the exclusive preserve of the medical profession and includes such people as social workers, marriage guidance counsellors, priests and those who run growth centres as well as the steadily increasing body of more or less trained 'alternative' therapists. Thus the scope that the discipline embraces has widened greatly, especially over the last twenty years, so that it encompasses not only those dealing with specific neuroses or psychological disorders which would naturally be treated by those with medical qualifications, but the much wider needs of those who seek some kind of meaning for their lives.

One can still, if one looks beneath the surface, find a confluence of aim in both views for the goal is, in a wide sense, to help the patient or client to be more effective by being more at one with the totality of himself or herself. If we try to see this development in perspective, and in particular take account of the needs I outlined in the last chapter, we can see two strands of thought at work. First, the relief of symptoms that trouble the patient so that he can cope more effectively with his life. Here the emphasis is on dealing with the world outside, through relationships and work in particular, by freeing the individual from the negative images that control him because of unconscious conflicts which originate in his past.

Second, helping the individual to fulfil himself more creatively and fully by looking inside and getting in touch with an intangible side of his nature which, whatever terminology is used, is effectively his 'spiritual' nature; and also, seeing the individual in terms of a wider social, and even universal, context, or as part of a greater whole.

We should now see that in answering one question, we are led to others which are more specific and that these questions are inevitably interrelated. And the more specific the questions, the more diversity we find. What is the psyche? What are the aims of the psychotherapist? What qualities are necessary for a psychotherapist? What sort of person will benefit from psychotherapy? Is psychotherapy a science or an art? These are questions that need to be asked, not so much to arrive at definite answers, of which there are probably none, but so that we can appreciate the problems that exist. It is all too easy to take these questions for granted and in doing so to adopt the intransigent attitudes that have unfortunately perpetuated the divisions that exist in the discipline today.

In the following sections of this chapter I shall look at some of the main streams of thought that have evolved. If we start with the basic aim of unity of the psyche, at the risk of over-simplification, we can go on from there to trace the different paths that have been taken. Wholeness necessarily entails uniting the different aspects of the psyche. Although it is generally

accepted, explicitly or implicitly, that the psyche is divided into
the unconscious and conscious sides, the main differences arise in
the nature, and consequently in the means of achieving union, of
these sides.

Freud, with his materialistic viewpoint, emphasized the
patient's need to cope with life in the world. He felt that if the
patient could be freed from the negative power of the
unconscious, then he would be in conscious control of his life and
so would be able to live a healthy and normal existence. The
method of achieving this aim was by drawing out the patient to
face himself through the medium of the therapist who acted as
neutral. The materialistic view assumes that there is no higher
dimension to the psyche and therefore that any apparent 'spiritual'
or creative aspiration is a sublimation of material instincts which
in turn assumes a negative nature of the unconscious which needs
to be re-directed into healthy channels. Thus if a person is helped
to form healthy and happy relationships and is content on the
material level he will have no need for any 'spiritual' needs.

The alternative view is that, far from being no more than a
material sublimation, the search for meaning is a real aspect of the
psyche's inherent need for unity with the positive nature of the
unconscious. According to this view, developed by Jung and held
by modern Humanist-Existential therapists, the aim of therapy is
to help the patient or client to deal with an inner void so that he
can become a creative person and find the identity he lacks. The
method of treatment also differs according to these ideas with the
therapist being a collaborator who draws out the patient by
becoming involved in an active relationship with him and the
personality of the therapist therefore assumes greater importance.

The limits of this approach have been reached with Carl Rogers
who has stated that it is the personality of the therapist alone that
matters. According to this view, provided the therapist has the
three essential qualities of: a caring attitude, empathy and
genuineness, the technique he employs, and incidentally his
training or lack of it, is irrelevant. This extreme view has

naturally provoked hostile reaction from the orthodox followers of Freud who have virulently condemned their colleagues as unscientific – a criticism which has also been levelled at Jung and his followers.

There is a great deal of justification for the view that much of the modern development of psychotherapy is unscientific. But this simply begs the question. Is psychotherapy a science or an art? And the further, no less important, question: 'What are the aims of therapy?' Are they to deal with specific mental illnesses or to help the individual to realize his potentials? Should therapy be concerned solely with relieving a patient's symptoms so that he can deal with the world more effectively or should it take account of a person's creative and spiritual needs?

There are those who argue that, whether or not these 'higher' needs of the psyche exist, they are in any event outside the scope of therapy, while others who argue that, if the individual is to be whole, then his needs as a whole must be taken into account. It should, I think, be clear from this brief survey, that what matters is the individual and his needs. Those who are concerned with helping their patients or clients to cope with their lives in the world are fulfilling their vocation and dealing with the very real problems that exist in people's lives. It may be that by their temperament they are incapable of recognizing the other needs that an individual may have. Equally, it may be perfectly valid to concentrate on the creative potentials of a particular individual if that is where his real needs lie, but that in turn is no reason for discounting the practical problems that exist for many, if not most, people.

2 The aims of psychotherapy

What is it that psychotherapists are trying to achieve? Before we turn in the next section to the different methods of achieving their aims, let us see if we can simplify matters by discovering an underlying objective, some common ground which is accepted by therapists as a body, no matter what terminology they may use or to which particular school or belief system they adhere.

I believe that there is a central objective which is shared by all therapists. That is not to detract from the very real differences that exist both in the models employed and in the methods of treatment used, nor even in the specific goals which are appropriate for particular individuals.

What then is this fundamental goal? It is to enable the patient to experience himself as a whole. This common objective, that of getting in touch with one's total being, has been termed 'self-realization' by Anthony Storr. He writes: 'I propose to call this final achievement self-realisation, by which I mean the fullest possible expression in life of the innate potentialities of the individual, the realisation of his own uniqueness as a personality.'[2]

Now wholeness necessarily implies division. For union to take place it must be accepted, explicitly or implicitly, that there are separate parts of the psyche. And it is at this point that different therapists begin to part company, and that their models differ. The earlier proponents of psychotherapy provided a model of the psyche which was clearly divided into two, these being effectively the conscious and the unconscious sides, even though those terms were not always used, or used in the same way.

The structure of the psyche was therefore based on that of nature itself as it was on the physical body. Life as we know it is dynamic, consisting of the interplay of opposing forces which create the conflicts within the human mind. The attempt to balance these inimical forces reflects the duality of the world itself where the principles of yang and yin, active and receptive, birth and death, light and dark oppose each other in their unending cycles. So it was that the term 'psycho-dynamic' was used to describe the early therapists and their followers.

The relative importance of the two sides varies considerably among practitioners. First, while accepting their existence, there is sharp divergence both as to their roles and their nature. Second, there are those who deny the very existence of the unconscious, but in concentrating wholly on the conscious side they necessarily imply another side – which is, in reality if not in name, the unconscious.

The first division, in the nature of the unconscious and the conscious, can be seen most clearly in the ideas of Freud and Jung respectively. Freud regarded the unconscious, or subconscious to use his original term, as something essentially negative. It was nature in the raw and contained those powerful forces which the individual was unable to face and which threatened to control him. His aim was to reverse this unhealthy situation so that the patient, through his conscious side, could control his unconscious. By tracing his conflicts back to their unconscious sources, the patient would be helped to free himself from their influence and the powers therein would be unblocked.

Freud's aim was to provide the patient with a positive self-image, to show him that he could succeed in the world, in relationships and in his work and his life as a whole so that he could function effectively. By enabling the patient, through his relationship with the therapist, to be freed from the past, he would be able to live in the present and cope with the future. In this way he would achieve wholeness by getting in touch with those parts of the psyche that were within his unconscious.

Jung's view of the unconscious was more positive than that of his mentor. Instead of regarding the unconscious as something that needed to be controlled and exorcised, he believed that it contained the real needs of the individual. By putting the patient in touch with his unconscious, he would find his real meaning in life. The emphasis in Jung's ideas was therefore both on the positive value of the unconscious as providing the individual's deeper goals and also in his concentration on the present rather than on the past.

Adler too, concentrated more on the present than on the past but he differed from his colleagues in emphasizing the importance of the conscious side. However, although he ostensibly denied the power, and even the existence, of the unconscious it is nevertheless implicit in his ideas that the two sides were contained in the psyche. The Humanist-Existential schools also place the emphasis on the present rather than the past and on the conscious rather than the unconscious. Their aim is to enable the patient to express himself, to become the person he really is, by taking responsibility for his own life and by freeing him from negative self-images. But when we look more closely at these views, it is implicit that the negative self-images arose from the past and that they are embedded in the unconscious.

Much of the division in practice between the protagonists of the different schools lies in their specific, as opposed to their general, aims, and also in the way that they seek to achieve these aims. Originally therapy was concerned with helping people to cope with their lives and thus with the outer world, for these people were suffering from specific problems and this underlay the initial derivation from medical practice. So Freud and his followers have been primarily concerned with helping people to deal with the practical problems of life. Such patients feel that they are failures; they are unable to have satisfactory relationships, to achieve in a career or even to cope with the normal aspects of life and the aim is to show the patient that he can succeed in the world. By unblocking the conscious side from the unconscious, by freeing the individual from his inner conflicts, he becomes integrated or whole.

With the gradual acceptance and development of the ideas of Jung and the modern existential therapists the emphasis has shifted towards the inner life. Here we can see a concentration on developing the individual's creative potentials, with the search for meaning, purpose and spiritual values. It should, however, be borne in mind first, that this shift did not invalidate the original aims but rather broadened the horizons of therapy by including them in their ambit, and in no way do they detract from those who do need to cope with the world. Second, these inner needs have always existed in some form. What can be seen here is that what had previously been the function of religion, philosophy and art had now become in addition, the province of the therapist.

It will, therefore, always be necessary to appreciate the needs of the individual and the fact that different people have different needs. Although it is true that everyone seeks wholeness and realization of his potentials and thus himself, there is a very real difference between those who need reinforcement to help them to cope with the world and those who need to experience inner meaning or spiritual values, and it is this divergence which to a large extent is reflected in the differing approach of therapists. The ability to appreciate the real needs of the individual and so the resistance of the temptation to assume too readily that his views coincide with the patient's is one that places the emphasis in practice as much on the personality as on the theoretical methods to which the therapist subscribes.

That in turn is why, in practice, the emphasis tends to be more on the therapist than the theory which he or she holds. As Anthony Storr has stated:

> It has long seemed to me that the analytical attitude to the patient is far more important then the school to which the analyst belongs; and that, in selecting a psychotherapist, it is more valuable to know whether he is capable of the right attitude to the patient than to know which theory of personality he holds.[3]

This view has been put in even more extreme form by Bloch: 'Technical expertise is secondary to this image of the therapist as a benign, kind and helpful person.'[4] In saying this it may appear that I am accepting the views of Carl Rogers that, provided the therapist is a congenial person it matters not whether he is trained or what technique he follows. I should therefore make it clear that training, and indeed technique, are of great importance, but that the healing process is brought about in the actual relationship between therapist and patient and that without the right qualities on the part of the therapist this healing will not take place.

This in turn brings us to the question of how the aims of the therapist are to be achieved, and so to the prerequisites which are necessary for therapy to be successful. These can be summarized in the following three basic requirements. First, there must be an intense, emotionally charged relationship between therapist and patient. To quote Bloch again: 'It is a well-established observation that a psychotherapy encounter devoid of emotion is highly unlikely to prove profitable.'[5] This was indeed the point that Rank made when he stated that it was in the emotional context of the relationship itself that healing took place rather than in the technique.

Second, there must be a rationale which provides an explanation of the problems and the means of resolving them. It follows that this rationale must be compatible with the shared views of the therapist and patient, even though the exact nature of the rationale is not in itself important provided that it gives the patient the sense of order he needs. Third, there must be a shared belief in the model used by the therapist and in the means of providing understanding. So the therapist must employ a model which means something to the patient, or to put it more bluntly, they must both be on the same wave-length.

It will be clear from this brief summary that there must be both an emotional and a rational meeting-point between therapist and patient and also a common form of belief system, or myth, for the healing process to take place. This will be of particular relevance when we come to look specifically at the role of astrology in therapy for here is one particular form of belief system. And it will also be clear when we look at the different schools and models in the next section that much of the divergence today stems from an inability to understand or accept different viewpoints and models, even though the underlying aims are in reality the same.

3 *Schools and models*

Therapy is different in every case.

CARL JUNG[6]

Much of the confusion that exists in the state of psychotherapy today is reflected in the different schools. With well over a hundred, and with more appearing all the time, it is difficult to keep track of them, yet alone find a coherent way of classifying them.

Any form of classification is largely a matter of convenience. As I am more concerned in this book with understanding the psyche through the symbolism of the Birth Chart so that the understanding may be used in therapy, I shall concentrate on the various theories of the psyche and its models rather than on either the targets or the goals of treatment.

So here I have adopted one generally accepted form of classification based on the schools. First, the Psychodynamic schools consisting of the founders of psychoanalysis, Freud and his immediate colleagues, Jung and Adler, and those who have followed these three. Second, the Humanist-Existentialist schools embracing, for example, the client-centred therapy of Carl Rogers, Gestalt therapy of Fritz Perls and Logotherapy of Victor Frankl. Third, and most briefly of all, the Behavioural school.

The Psychodynamic School consists first of Freud and his immediate followers and secondly the followers of Freud's original colleagues – Jung and Adler. The model which is common to all members of this group is that of a psyche which is divided into an unconscious and a conscious side. This essential division inevitably produces a sense of conflict within the individual and the therapist's goal is to enable the patient to experience this conflict by bringing into consciousness that which previously remained in the unconscious through an emotionally charged relationship which is implicit in the relationship between therapist and patient.

The actual model varies in emphasis between those who follow Freud's original ideas and those who have developed in other directions. Let us begin this outline by looking first at Freud himself and then at the other members of the group. Freud postulated the thesis that mental life is a product of the interaction of three psychic forces – the Ego, the Id, and the Superego.

He defined the Ego as the 'co-ordinated organisation of the mental processes in a person,' which perceives and makes sense of the environment, including both the internal psychological environment and the external world. Thus the Ego represents the executive part of the psyche, whose function it is to establish what can and what cannot be achieved and what kinds of wishes can be fulfilled. He regarded the Id as the unconscious, the seat of repressed feelings, fantasies and drives. It is the Id which is the dominant force in early childhood, while the Ego gradually becomes more important. Thus as the Ego gains ascendancy over the Id, the pleasure principle gives way to the reality principle and so the individual is freed from his primitive, instinctual drives and is enabled to act rationally.

The third aspect of the psyche, the Superego, is the moral agency which acts as the conscience, or ego-ideal, of the individual, the type of person he strives to become. It develops mainly as the child assimilates the moral precepts of its parents. The task of the Ego is to provide equilibrium between these three aspects of the psyche and it is the Ego's failure to cope satisfactorily which leads to neurotic symptoms. Thus the Ego has to contend with, control, and integrate the three forces for the satisfaction of the individual.

Freud believed that everything exists in mental images – ourselves, our parents, men, women, other people. It is these images, which are inevitably subjective as they reside in the individual mind or psyche, that need to be understood and that are thus the subject of the therapeutic process. What is necessary, according to Freud's view, is that the patient should experience the reality of these images for himself and the purpose of therapy is therefore to enable the patient to experience the conflicts that exist in these images by the technique of free association.

Problems arise because the patient is unable to live his own life as a result of his negative self-images and so these negative images need to be unblocked. Therefore, in Freud's words: 'When we can help a disturbed personality to outgrow the blocking effects of its internal conflicts, we can trust the normal development process to take over.' Implicit in this view is the idea that the psyche is self-regulating, and in common with the rest of nature and the physical body, it has a tendency towards balance. Balance is unattainable initially because of the unconscious blockages. Once these have been removed, the psyche will of its own accord revert to its proper state of equilibrium.

The way to achieve this unblocking is to go back to the original causes of the trouble, in other words to the origins of the images. These have been laid down in the Superego which created the ego ideal. Thus the images are derived in the Superego through the unconscious images of the parents and their successors. In this way the lessons are learned in the early life of the individual and it is these which thereafter decide his behaviour.

The point here is that until these unconscious images are brought out into the open the patient will continue to be bound by them and his life will be controlled by them. Neurosis occurs when the conflicts within the unconscious disturb the equilibrium of the three forces by trying to break through to the surface. Thus Freud regarded the neurotic symptoms as the Ego's attempt to adapt to the conflict by discharging the anxiety that ensues and restoring the psyche's balance. However, although neurosis can thus be seen as the psyche's attempt to heal itself, simply bringing the problems out into the open will not necessarily effect a cure, for the resulting crisis may fail to be resolved.

What happens in Freudian thereapy is that the patient is taught to experience the conflict for himself. He uses the therapist as a blank screen and transfers his own feelings onto him. The therapist then interprets the resultant 'transference neurosis' which is a transitional state between the original neurotic condition and normal psychological functioning. In this way the patient learns to experience his conflicts for himself and by unblocking these conflicts the unconscious is made conscious as well as acceptable and accessible to the Ego.

In spite of the growth of alternative methods of treatment and
the theories that have proliferated since Freud first put forward his
ideas, the vast majority of practising therapists still accept his basic
views. Many, indeed, have succeeded in sticking so rigidly to his
original ideas that they have refused to accept the subsequent
development of his own ideas. Other practitioners have retained
the basic psychoanalytical approach of Freud but have developed
an emphasis in other directions. Karen Horney and H. S. Sullivan,
for example, laid particular emphasis on social factors in
behaviour. And Otto Rank, one of Freud's most faithful adherents,
regarded the emotional events incorporated into the actual
treatment in psychoanalysis as the effective agent rather than the
emergence of the contents of the unconscious itself.

Melanie Klein, as a neo-Freudian, parted company with Freud
in emphasizing the difficulties encountered in the first weeks or
months of childhood. She felt that the experiences of this early
period were not only significant in the development of the
individual, but were pre-eminent over later experience. Thus in
her view it was necessary to investigate the early stages of
infantile anxiety and aggressiveness, and it was the aggressive
drives which she believed to be of particular importance. As the
first experience of a child centres round the mother, she believed
that the early childhood projections and introjections are derived
from her.

In her view the feelings and attitudes which are originally
associated with significant figures and especially the mother, are
later transferred to others and they then play a vital role in the
individual's self-image and his relationships. So if a child is
sufficiently loved by his parents, he will feel significant and will be
able to relate normally to other people. In these circumstances he
will never question the point of life or the meaning of existence.
In this latter conclusion can be seen a very important divergence
between the original Freudian ideas and the later development of
Jung and others. For Jung believed that the search for meaning
was inherent in the psyche, while the Freudians, with their

materialistic assumptions, saw it only as a sublimation of or compensation for the inability to relate.

Still continuing in the Freudian tradition, Karen Horney placed the emphasis on solving current conflicts while accepting the vital role of love in the life of a young child. She believed that anxiety is produced by the original state of helplessness of the child which, if not adequately developed, can produce one of three defective patterns of relating. The child may either move towards others, adopting a helpless submissive attitude in an attempt to gain affection, or he will move against others, in an attempt to conquer a hostile world, or he will move away from others and withdraw from society. The therapist's aim, according to this view, is to help the patient move with others so that he can form relationships which are reciprocal and mutual, and thus attain a greater level of self-realization.

Eric Berne apparently parted company with Freud by concentrating on the present rather than on the past. He believed that the individual is in charge of his own destiny and that his aim is to attain autonomy so that he can be himself and cope with life. However, he accepted Freud's basic ideas that the roots of present conflicts lie in the past and are derived from the patient's treatment by his parents and other significant people. In his view at the root of all behaviour is the desire to be loved and it is in accordance with the child's early treatment that he is led to question whether or not he deserves to be loved.

If the individual does not believe he deserves this love he will work out ways to achieve it and these ways, which are constantly repeated, become a form of conditionig which Berne termed the person's script and which in turn develop into a game he plays in life. The games inevitably fail because the individual is trying to resolve his inner conflicts which sprung from his own past through another person. Once he becomes aware of his negative decisions, then he can rewrite his script and attain the three conditions of autonomy: awareness, spontaneity and intimacy.

Berne's resultant therapy, through Transactional Analysis, consists of setting definite goals for the patient to achieve, making contracts with him which include specific changes in his behaviour, and thus the emphasis is firmly on the patient accepting responsibility for his life and his decisions. This goal is implicit in Berne's concept of the three Ego states: parent, adult and child, for when the patient finally succeeds in taking responsibility he can act as an adult.

Two of Freud's original colleagues, Jung and Adler, founded major schools of their own. The ideas of Alfred Adler were founded on the thesis that the individual strives to be powerful in order to compensate for an original inferiority complex. So it is the very inferiority of the individual's functions which stimulate him to overcome his defect, enabling the inferior function to become the superior one. Because of organic or psychological problems which result in lowered self-esteem an intense struggle for self-assertion takes place. Therefore the goal is social significance or power. This emphasis, not only on power, but on the social context of the individual sprung from Adler's own background both as the son of a Jewish outsider who had been converted to Protestantism and a physical defect resulting from his contracting pneumonia at the age of five.

Adler saw the character as a set of attitudes which have been adapted by the individual to deal with the various types of situation to which he is exposed. So the traits which he produces are adapted because of their functional value to him in the earliest years of his life, and these traits are those which appeared to give the best results in terms of power, in the particular setting in which he was placed. Although Adler did not use the terms 'conscious' and 'unconscious' and insisted on concentrating on the present and the future, rather than on the past, his view that the real aims of the individual could be seen by his actual behaviour rather than what he thinks they are, implied the division into unconscious and conscious, for his *real* aims were necessarily unconscious.

Moreover, the division was implicit as much in the actual behaviour of the individual as in his real goal. Adler stated that there are three ways of coping with a person's striving for superiority. The first, and successful one, is compensation where striving leads to the satisfactory adjustment to the three challenges of life: society, work and sex. However, if the individual fails to cope with his basic feeling of inferiority, he assumes a false self, and the resultant neurosis may take the form either of overcompensation, where the striving becomes too apparent and there is maladjustment, for example a weak person who becomes a criminal like the effeminate Heydrich or the bureaucratic Himmler. Alternatively, the individual retreats into illness in order to obtain power.

Although Adler is now given little overt credit in the development of psychotherapy, his ideas have been accepted to a much wider extent than is generally recognized. In that the individual is now seen more as part of a greater whole, whether it be his own family or as part of a wider social community, he can be regarded as the true founder of community mental health. And in stressing the importance of the present and future, he can be seen as the first exponent of the humanist-existential movement.

While Adler is now largely neglected of the original three, Jung's heritage can be seen in an extreme form. At one end of the spectrum, many traditional psychoanalysts regard him as a heretic and a freak, interested more in spiritual pursuits than real therapy, while at the other extreme, he is regarded as a guru figure and the apotheosis of a new cult by the alternative movements. Both attitudes would have caused no little surprise to Jung who regarded himself as empirical and resisted the formation of his own school until comparatively late in life.

Jung's major departure from orthodox Freudian thought lay in his positive regard for the unconscious side of the psyche, as well as in his views of the unconscious itself. While Freud saw the unconscious, or subconscious, as something essentially negative which needed to be controlled by the conscious Ego, Jung regarded conscious and unconscious more as two equal partners. And the emphasis here was in bringing out the unconscious, where the real needs of the individual lay, so that a state of equilibrium could be achieved. From this point of view it can be seen that a neurosis often serves a positive function, for it may be derived as an attempt by the unconscious to compensate for a one-sided, unhealthy, conscious attitude.

But it should not be assumed that every individual's need lies in getting in touch with his unconscious side. The aim for everyone is balance. Where consciousness has developed too far, and where the Ego is strong enough to cope with the contents of the unconscious, then the process of facing the unconscious and reconciling it to the conscious side can take place. This process Jung termed 'individuation' but he made it clear that the individuation process is one that is applicable only to a few.

This is something that needs to be stressed because unfortunately many of those who have adhered so readily to Jung's views fail to appreciate this basic prerequisite. Jung himself stated quite clearly:

> It is appropriate only in those cases where consciousness has reached an abnormal degree of development and has diverged too far from the unconscious.... For the same reasons, this way of development has scarcely any meaning before the middle of life (normally between the ages of thirty-five and forty), and if entered upon too soon can be decidedly injurious.[7]

Jung, then, held the view that consciousness evolved from unconsciousness and that therefore it was in the unconscious that man could trace his roots and find his deepest needs. The whole of the psyche consists both of the unconscious and the conscious which has developed from it, and the aim is for the conscious side, or the Ego, to get in touch with the unconscious. The relative importance between these two sides led to a consequent divergence in both the aim and the method of therapy, and indeed with regard to the kind of person to whom such therapy was directed.

The aim was to find the individual's creative potential, or to discover meaning within his life, and the means was through a sharing and collaborative relationship between therapist and patient, rather than specifically through transference and counter-transference. The aim inevitably reflected the type of patient who was a person who, having succeeded in the first half of his life in the world, was faced in the second with a sense of meaninglessness. Much of the criticism that has been directed at Jung from Freudians is because the latter fail to appreciate the aims that Jung was trying to meet, or more specifically, who feel that these aims are beyond the scope of therapy.

Jung did of course believe, as Freud did not, that everyone needs, in searching for meaning, a spiritual quality to their lives, and that this spiritual quality was an integral aspect of the psyche. Here there was a definite divergence between Freud and Jung, for Freud believed that if people were happy in the material world they would have no reason to seek meaning outside and that any such search was no more than a sublimation of the material, and usually the sexual, urge which for some reason could not find normal release. Anthony Storr has paraphrased the position in these words: 'Freud undoubtedly attributed supreme value to the orgastic release of sex, whereas Jung found supreme value in the unifying experience of religion.'[8]

However, as the passage I have quoted above shows, Jung made it abundantly clear that the majority of people do not question the meaning of life and, moreover, that most people should not question it. Similarly, there is a clear divergence in Jung's views in the general and the individual. He in any case, in common with Adler, believed in the importance of society, and he was concerned with the general need of society in his age for a sense of meaning beyond the material. I think that whatever view one takes of the individual's needs it would be hard to deny the existential vacuum, the sense of alienation and purposelessness that has steadily prevailed in recent times. Freud of course began his work not only from a different premise to Jung, but also in a society that was more structured. By the time Jung was developing his ideas this structure was breaking down and he felt, rightly or wrongly, that this greater need of society was a factor that should be taken into account in psychotherapy.

Nevertheless, when he dealt with individual patients he would take account of their particular needs, and if they were based on unresolved images from the past he was not averse to dealing with them along more orthodox Freudian lines. From the wider context of Jung's work, he could as well be classified along with the Humanist-Existential tradition which we shall now briefly examine, or alternatively he could be seen as a bridge between the past and present.

What has come to be known as the Humanist-Existential School, and which in reality is a group of theories connected by certain common viewpoints, came into being as a reaction against Freud's instinct-based, unconscious determinism. Its basic tenets are: first, that everyone is the author of his own world, and second, that knowledge of this world can only be achieved by experiencing it with his consciousness.

This school is based on the ideas of existential philosophy and in many ways can be seen as a mixture, in practice if not in theory, of the ideas of Adler and Jung. Inasmuch as it concentrates on consciousness and the present, it owes much of its impetus to Adler, while in focusing on the search for meaning it looks to Jung. The philosophy of existentialism is based on the inevitability of death, the freedom to choose and act, the need to take responsibility for one's life and the centrality of meaningfulness and purpose. According to these premises the basic need is to face the emptiness, the void, or lack of meaning that exists within the individual.

And in order to experience his world, the patient goes through a process of confrontation and encounter where he faces three aspects of the world – first, the environment and the biological possibilities of a human being; second, the world and his relationships with other people; and third, the world of his own inner experience. When one looks at the related theories that are shared by these schools one can see that the central aim is to enable the individual to become his own self by facing his real nature. And when one looks beneath the surface of the theoretical concepts one sees also that this aim is one that is shared in essence by all therapists. Where the real difference arises is in the way the patient can get in touch with this 'real' self and, to a lesser extent, of what this 'real' self consists.

The major divergence that one sees when one looks at treatment is that instead of the therapist taking a neutral stance – a sounding board which reflects the unconscious conflicts of the patient – he takes an active role in treatment. For here is is accepted that the patient can know the world only through actively experiencing it by his own consciousness and the therapist must help the patient to face his real self by accepting him and enforcing his feeling of self-worth. This, of course, is why in this school it is the personality of the therapist which is so much more important than the technique he employs.

It is here accepted that there is an inherent difference between the Self and Self-concepts. The Self obeys natural laws while Self-concepts limit and produce conflicts of the natural organism. As the individual introjects and internalizes other people's values in order to achieve positive regard from others his own feelings of self-worth are lessened because he realizes that he cannot meet outside expectations, nor can he fulfil his own expectations. Furthermore, the negative self-concepts induce behaviour which reinforces the image of inadequacy and worthlessness.

Thus psychological disturbance arises as a result of the blocking of the authenticity process. The patient pursues goals which are not his own, which are determined externally instead of answering internal needs. Therapy, then, consists of accepting the client, this term being generally preferred to that of patient, as he is in the present and to provide him with a feeling of self-worth by building up his confidence in himself and by encouraging him to rely on his inner self and reality.

In accepting the individual as part of a greater whole these ideas are in accordance with modern thought for they are based on the holistic view of the individual and his relationship with his environment, and in concentrating on the present in order to encourage a state of self-reliance the emphasis is shifted on the client rather than the therapist. In Gestalt therapy the psyche's dynamic, rhythmic role is emphasized as part of a natural process so that the client can distinguish between the negative pattern of self-images and his real needs which continue to assert themselves.

The goals which are shared by Carl Rogers's client-centred therapy, Fritz Perls's Gestalt therapy and Viktor Frankl's Logotherapy and the Encounter groups, are to promote an expanded appreciation of the client's situation in the world so that he becomes more spontaneous, responsible for his life and actions, aware of personal meaning and purpose and his creative potential so that he is able to exploit it, become open to new experience and free to grow. The vital relationship between therapist and client is one based on collaboration and shared venture. Thus it is the way the therapist accepts the client, and what the therapist is rather than what he does, that is of ultimate importance.

The reaction against Freud's original ideas was a healthy sign of a developing science. Any meaningful discipline should proceed in accordance with current ideas and beliefs if it is to reflect the needs that exist in a dynamic society. In putting forward new ideas there will always be a tendency to reject much of the old which may still be valid and it is easy for divisions to become polarized. It then becomes necessary to look objectively at the state of the discipline as a whole in order to see it in perspective.

The greatest impetus for modern therapy has come from the USA with such protagonists as Rollo May, Abraham Maslow's 'third force' and Gordon Allport, apart from those mentioned above. In western Europe Ludwig Binswanger, Medard Boss,

Roland Kuhn, Roberto Assagioli, as well as Victor Frankl, have led the movement while in Britain Robert Laing has been the main exponent until recent times although the influences from the USA and Europe have grown steadily stronger among 'alternative' practitioners.

Let us at this point try to integrate the main ideas by looking beneath the surface and trying to find some central theme. The basic tenet of humanist psychology is that the lived experience of a person is the only criterion of truth. This puts the emphasis firmly on the present so that the individual takes responsibility for his own life and it also places the emphasis on consciousness so that the client can participate actively in his life to live out his creative needs as an individual and as an integral part of society as a whole, both in respect of his immediate environment and in terms of his fellow human beings and indeed as part of the universe.

We can see here the main divergence from Freud's tendency to look back to the past although the emphasis on consciousness also effectively devalues Jung's belief in the central importance of the unconscious. When, however, we look more deeply at the situation, it is clear that the aim is still the same – that of getting in touch with oneself. The major departure, in reality if not in language and emphasis, lies not so much with the underlying aim, as in the means to achieve the common goal.

Freud was also trying to help his patients to live in the present and to be responsible for their lives, but he believed that it was necessary, to achieve this end, to go back into the past in order to free the patient from the unconscious blockages which had occurred. Indeed when one looks at Carl Rogers's non-directive therapy, for example, one can see the equivalent of Freud's original negative images created by the Super-ego, in Rogers's differentiation between the Self and the negative Self-concepts which limit and produce conflicts in the natural organism.

To a great extent the appropriate therapy will depend on the patient and his needs, the point that Jung was at such pains to point out. And in practice this is why the modern therapies are more appropriate for those who want to live more creative, meaningful lives as opposed to those who suffer from specific neuroses. The important point is to recognize where the conflicts that exist in the individual patient or client lie and then to approach them either in the present or in the past. For some, the freedom they achieve from the blockages which originated in their past will enable them to cope effectively with their lives, and the inherent self-regulation of the psyche that Freud postulated will produce equilibrium. For others the conflicts need to be transformed into creative channels to provide them with the sense of meaning and purpose they seek to achieve – that wholeness which lies in the unity of their conflicts.

The Behavioural School also concentrates on the present but its premise is materialistic rather than creative. It holds that all human behaviour is learned and that neurotic symptoms are examples of maladaptive behaviour which result when faulty learning has taken place. The goal of treatment here is then to unlearn specific patterns of behaviour which, having been laid down, continue to attract the individual to the same kind of situations, and replace them, through new learning, with more adaptive patterns.

In this case the therapist is concerned with where and when the problem arises and what it is that maintains it. He is not concerned with why the problem exists or how it came into being. The problem is then identified, the therapist makes a contract with the patient to solve it and ensures that the patient is responsible for his cure. It should be clear that the Behavioural School is goal-orientated and based firmly on the present. Consciousness alone is regarded as relevant and specific problems, like phobias, obsessions, compulsions are those which are most commonly the subject of its treatment.

In stating that all human behaviour is learned one can see the development of the Behavioural School from Freudian concepts, but it is only fair to say that practitioners of this School are more concerned with specific problems than theoretical models of the psyche. One can also see the influence, or at least confluence, of Berne's ideas in the attempt to enable the patient to unlearn his behaviour patterns which is akin to Berne's aim of getting his patients to 're-write' their scripts.

But in concentrating on the problem areas themselves, rather than their causes, the emphasis is in the same direction as the modern schools, even though the underlying concepts are different. Certainly the aim is to help the patient to be self-reliant and therapy consists of the therapist acting in collaboration with the patient. However, as the problems tend to be specific ones, this school, important as it may be in itself, is inevitably limited and cannot deal with more general questions of the human psyche.

4 *Psychotherapy and astrology*

> The problem with the human race is that it consists of human beings.
>
> PASCAL

From the outline I have just given, it will be apparent that there are major differences in outlook in psychotherapy today as well as basic aims which are common to all practitioners. It will also be clear that certain approaches are more appropriate for certain therapists and patients or clients. What must always be borne in mind is that it is the essence of the individual which we are trying to reach. It is this essence or 'spirit' which each individual needs to become in order to live his or her own life.

The models that are used in the different therapeutic schools are, like any other models, convenient tools. We need to use them because we cannot see the human psyche directly. We cannot see the spirit. But all the models describe the same underlying entity and, because it is impossible to see the psyche directly, these models will never be totally accurate.

While it is important to be aware of the situation in psychotherapy in order to understand the psyche better and in order to learn the techniques of therapy, it must also be appreciated that the Horoscope in astrology is a model which is just as meaningful as any model that the various schools of psychotherapy provide. It is not a question of correlating the Birth Chart with a particular psychological model but rather of learning to use the Horoscope as a symbol in its own right in order to understand and get in touch with the psyche that is reflected therein.

The Horoscope is in fact the most effective symbol of the psyche. First, because its symbolic language is far richer than any that can be found in the various schools of therapy. And second, because it is the only symbol that exists of each individual human psyche that is born into the world. The Horoscope is thus unique as a means of perceiving the reality under the surface and it is important that astrologers, while learning the techniques of psychotherapy, use the Horoscope itself as a direct means of access to the individual it represents.

Having looked at the different schools and methods it should be clear that the differences of viewpoint lie not so much in the cause of the problems or even so much in the nature of the problems but rather in the most appropriate way of dealing with them. Whatever terminology is used it is generally accepted that, because of external influences being introjected by the individual, a conflict arises between his real self and the false images that result from these influences. Certainly there is a difference in the way these external images are seen – Freud believing them to be purely personal, in other words as a result only of the actual parents or other significant people in the child's early life. There is also some difference of opinion among Neo-Freudians as to the relative importance of these influences both in the strength of parental importance and in the age when they are relevant, while Jung believed that they are common to everyone and resided in what he termed the 'collective unconscious'.

Therefore it is generally accepted that the roots of the problems lie in the divergence contained within these early influences and that these influences are the result of the way the child viewed his parents, or whoever took their place in practice. However, when it comes to dealing with the resultant problems, or deciding how to enable the individual to be himself, there is a conflict not only between the appropriate methods but in particular in deciding which point of contact is relevant.

Freud was concerned with freeing the patient from his past by going back to the origins of his problems which lay in the past. He believed that once the unconscious conflicts were unblocked the natural equilibrium of the psyche would take over and the healing process could take place. But this treatment is appropriate mainly for those who suffer from specific neuroses and Freud took the view that the neurosis could only be healed if the patient lived through it. If he succeeded in doing this then he would no longer be troubled by the past and he could live his own life and cope with relationships and the practical matters of the world.

The Behaviourists, while accepting that the origins of the problems lie in the past, are more concerned with dealing with specific kinds of problems in the present. Many of the modern schools also are more concerned with attacking the problems in the present rather than in the past, for they believe that this is the only way to help people to take responsibility for their lives. Once again what is important is what the real needs of the individual are. Here one can only look at the individual. However much a person may need to live in the present it may be necessary for him to face something in his past while for others the past may be irrelevant.

I emphasize these points because they are important not only for therapists but particularly for the astrologer who uses his discipline in therapy. It is all too easy to get attached to the model of the psyche rather than understanding the individual which that model represents. Astrologers as a whole will be more likely to be concerned with those whose needs lie in the direction of inner purpose and meaning but there will also be many whose real needs are in dealing with the practical matters of the world.

This tendency is apparent with the accent on Jung and many of the modern schools today. Although Jung was concerned in particular with a deeper sense of meaning and purpose, he specifically stated:

> A doctor must be familiar with the so-called 'methods'. But he must guard against falling into any specific routine approach. In general one must guard against theoretical assumptions. Today they may be valid, tomorrow it may be the turn of other assumptions. In my analyses they play no part. I am unsystematic very much by intention. To my mind, in dealing with individuals, only individual understanding will do. We need a different language for every patient. In one analysis I can be heard talking the Adlerian dialect, in another the Freudian.[9]

We have already noted the prerequisites that are necessary for the therapist–patient relationship to take place. Let us now see how these apply specifically to the astrotherapist. First, there must be an emotionally charged relationship between therapist and patient. This qualification is of particular importance for the astrologer and it is, I believe, the reason why the practice so often fails to fulfil the theory. The client needs to reach his unconscious and this must be achieved through the symbolism of the Birth Chart. An approach which is purely rational will never work. The symbolic approach is one that is intuitive. The therapist talks of the conscious and unconscious. The astrologer sees the Sun and the Moon. There he can see both the general and the particular. These two primary energies symbolize the two sides of the psyche. Whether they are described as the masculine and feminine sides, as the animus and anima, or as the introjected parental images, the principles remain the same.

Second, there must be a rationale which is acceptable to the client. And here, too, astrology provides the ideal vehicle because it contains the only model of the individual psyche which can be approached rationally. We have already noted the lack of such a model in psychology. The point of such a rationale is to provide the patient with a sense of order, and the fact that it is not totally consistent is relatively unimportant. Astrology therefore provides a language which astrologer and client can share, one that means something to both.

This condition leads necessarily to the final prerequisite, the need for a system in which both therapist and client believe. No one can be forced unwillingly to solve either his specific problems or to realize himself as a creative human being. Some patients will, because of their inherent temperament, be attracted to one form of therapy but will find another inimical. Similarly the client must believe in astrology – otherwise there will be no real relationship which can provide the basis for treatment. Given these conditions the Horoscope will provide the basis for treatment whereby the client can begin to experience his real self.

CHAPTER 3

The astrology of eternity – the Kabbalah and the ideal Psyche

1 *The universal Horoscope – the Tree of Life*

To him that overcometh will I give to eat of the tree of life, which is in the midst of the paradise of God.

REVELATIONS 2:7

The goal in psychotherapy is harmony. This state of harmony, the balance which is the ideal of each psyche, is symbolized in the Tree of Life in the system of the Kabbalah. While the Horoscope provides the model of the individual psyche, reflecting the moment that each human being is born into the world, the Tree of Life is the model of the same psyche in its ideal state, reflecting the wholeness to which it is irresistibly drawn.

The process of therapy lies in healing the psyche, of making it whole. The state of wholeness is implicit within the psyche as it is in every form of life because each created thing begins in unity. The inherent force that draws us towards that unity can be seen both in the need to relate to some entity outside ourselves and in the need to contain the various attributes that are the result of the division of that original unity.

Each individual psyche needs to find its own unity, the path that each of us must follow is ours alone and it is symbolized in the separate moment of time that is our Birth Chart. Equally the goal is the same for all of us; every path leads to the centre. In the Tree we see the complete cyclic process of time which unites the separate moments of individual birth, that which we call eternity, reflecting the universe as a single organism. The Tree, then, is the goal which we never attain, the Grail which we never fail to seek, the Kingdom. The Horoscope is the path from which we never escape, the way that the King must travel. The paradox of life is that the two are the same. The Temple of God is within us; the King journeys through life searching for his Kingdom which, like the original tree in Paradise, is always beside him.

The problem of uniting the psyche, of making the patient or client whole, is one that is common both to the therapist and the astrologer. First, there is the general problem of union which implies a division into two and which in therapy is generally regarded as a split between the conscious and unconscious sides of the psyche. Second, there is the specific problem of understanding the complexes and conflicts that exist in the individual psyche.

In lacking either a model of the individual psyche or a consistent model of the ideal psyche, the psychotherapist is faced with an initial disadvantage. Astrologers have, in the Horoscope, a model of the individual psyche but when we look at these planetary energies in the Horoscope we tend to see them in isolation for there is no natural connection between them. By looking at the same energies on the Tree we can see them as parts of the whole in their natural state, for not only do they flow from each other but they are each connected with each other by the twenty-two paths of the Tarot major arcana.

When we combine Astrology with the Kabbalah as parts of the one system they are we find in the latter the natural complement of the former. In both the Tree of Life and the Horoscope we have a model of the human psyche where unity is broken down into ten principles – in the Horoscope there are the Sun, the Moon and the eight planets, while on the Tree there are the sephiroth. The difference between the two models is that in the Tree we see their intrinsic state where each separate principle forms a connection with each of the other principles to provide a perfect, immutable, balanced pattern, while in the Horoscope these same principles are arranged apparently at random and there is thus no inherent connection between the separate factors.

Therefore in astrology we tend to regard the Sun, Moon and

planets as separate energies each representing some diverse principle of the human psyche: Mars, the assertive energy, Saturn, the principle of inhibition, and Jupiter, the need or ability for expansion. Now, so far as it goes this is a valid way of seeing the parts. But it must also be appreciated that the parts are not only parts – they are in essence parts of the whole. When we look at the same energies on the Tree we can see the unity. We can see first, how each principle evolves from its predecessor according to its innate number and second, how each is balanced by the others. Then we see that the apparently independent principles are no more separate in reality than the moment of time when we are born – each is a part of a greater whole.

In this way we learn to perceive ourselves as we are, as a whole, and also as belonging to the greater wholes that constitute our fellow men and women, all other forms of life, the universe and God who created all in His image. Then, too, we perceive the fundamental fact that unity and division are the same. Unity is the whole organism, whether it is the universe, or God, or the individual psyche, or any other thing. The rest, the divisions which are symbolized by the planets and the sephiroth, are attributes or forms of this oneness; according to Aristotle they constitute the ten modes of life. Because we cannot perceive the unity, because we cannot see God directly or His spirit which resides in us, the essential unity is manifested to us in differentiation and thus it is only the differentiation that we are aware of with our normal senses.

There are two needs that every psyche shares, two ways each psyche needs to unite. The first reflects the initial division of the one into the two. Thus therapists as a whole accept the need to unite the conscious and unconscious sides. What distinguishes them is in the method of achieving this union, and the division between therapists is effectively a choice between uniting with something outside through relationships or work, or, on the other hand, relating with something inside – with the other side of one's own psyche through purpose or meaning.

When we look at the primary division of the Tree illustrated in Figure 3.1 we see two pillars which represent these two sides and I shall look at these in detail in the next section of this chapter. Second, we see the division into the ten principles symbolized in the systems of Astrology and the Kabbalah. These I shall look at in detail in the last section of this chapter. The need here is to experience all that is within us in order to achieve the harmony that is the psyche's goal.

2 *The pillars of manifestation – the harmony of the Psyche*

> Know ye not that ye are the temple of God, and that
> the Spirit of God dwelleth in you?
>
> 1 CORINTHIANS 3:16

The psyche seeks balance as its ultimate goal. This is not a goal that can ever be achieved in this life of ours and thus life consists not of reaching the goal but of the journey towards that goal. This indeed is the paradox that we call life. All life, as well as our own human existence, is a conflict between two opposing forces and these forces need to be accepted and contained within us.

The dual nature of life has always been recognized. In the east we have the symbol of the Tao whose two halves flow the one into the other, and whose essence is contained within each other. This symbol enables us to see, not only that the opposites exist, separate and yet integral parts of each other, but moreover that the one emanates from the other as part of an inherent cyclic process. So the dawn unfolds imperceptibly, beckoning the new day, the hope of spring encroaches as winter dies and the leaves decay at the end of summer presaging the darkening woods of autumn.

The division in the west is sharper. The two pillars of the temple stand apart – Boaz on the left, Jachin on the right, the light and the dark, the warring forces of the world, the bright, midday sword of Michael slaying the subtle dragon of Satan. Good and evil, God and Devil, male and female, spirit and body, Heaven

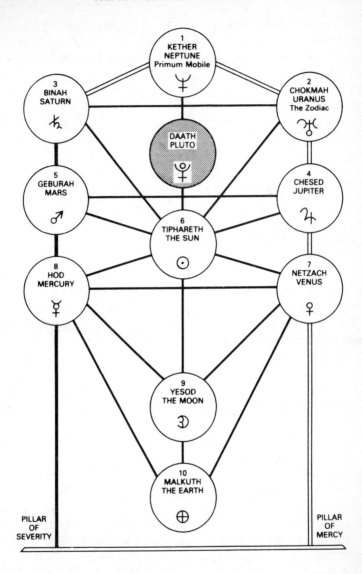

Figure 3.1   *The Tree of Life – the sephiroth and the planets*

and Earth. But the two are contained as equal partners within the basic symbol of all life, of every human psyche, of each form of existence that is symbolized in the Tree of Life.

And this symbol, therefore, serves as a constant reminder that both forces are equal aspects of each one of us. In Figure 3.1 we can see that the ten sephiroth, and another which is invisible, are all placed vertically in three columns. Strictly speaking the left and the right form the two pillars of the Temple and on a physical level they correspond with the two sides of the body. The middle column represents the principle of balance or equilibrium itself and its function is to synthesize the pillars.

This will be apparent as we look at the sephiroth. For the time being we can bear in mind that the sephiroth on the pillars themselves represent the planets, and the Zodiac itself, while on the middle column we have, from the bottom up, the Earth, the Moon, the Sun, through the invisible sephira, until we reach the Crown which is nameless. Thus we have the opposites facing each other with unity in the middle, or the reconciliation of the opposing principles.

Here, too, we can see the natural order of things – how each separate energy combines with the others. And in this way it is made clear that the energies themselves, in the form of planets or sephiroth, are not isolated forms of being, but obtain their meaning from the whole. So some energies balance each other directly, like Mars and Jupiter which oppose each other on the Tree, while others balance each other indirectly. Mars, for example, being between Saturn and Mercury on a vertical line and opposing Venus diagonally across the Tree, finding its resolution in the Sun which lies between the two. Furthermore, the precise nature of the links between the energies is contained in the symbolism of the twenty-two paths which correspond with the major arcana of the Tarot. Thus the path connecting Mars with the Sun is Justice while that which connects Jupiter with the Sun is the Hermit.

The inherent connection between these separate energies, the parts which make up the whole, which in astrology are symbolized by the planets, is something which can only be seen on the Tree. In the Horoscope we see the energies as they are placed in each individual human psyche. The integrity of the psyche in its ideal form is that which is contained on the Tree and here too we can see the unity, not only of the human psyche, but of life as a whole.

This is of the utmost importance if we are concerned with wholeness, for wholeness means not only being whole ourselves but also recognizing that we are part of a greater whole. So we can see that the two opposing principles – whether we call them the light and the dark, good and evil, yin and yang, active and receptive – are contained equally within us and within the whole of life. This is why God and Man are the same in essence and why the one reflects the other.

The principle of the opposites is contained, not only in the pillars, but in the sephiroth themselves as they stand on the pillars. So when we look at the sephiroth in terms of numbers we can see that although in themselves they are active and passive alternatively, depending on whether they are odd or even respectively, the principle of activity and receptiveness is also contained within each number. For example, the 3, Binah or Saturn, receives the 2 as form – the womb or the Great Mother receiving the yod or sperm of Chokmah or Uranus, and then it establishes its active side in relation to the following number. So, as the 3, it provides the force which infuses the form of the 4, Chesed or Jupiter, which becomes the first solid structure.

The principle of creation from unity, manifestation in duality, synthesis in the birth of union in the 3 and then the destruction of that pattern in the 4, which from within itself begins a further cycle of creation, manifestation, birth and death can also be seen throughout the sephiroth starting at the top until the final resolution at the bottom of the Tree.

This principle is one that goes back to early occult philosophy and is readily apparent in the four aspects of God which are incorporated in the Tetragrammaton – the Holy Name of God. It is upon this principle that the continuous cycles of change are based. First, there is the active principle, the act of creation, the first Yod, or divine spark which begins the cycle. Then the passive principle, the Hé, which receives this creative principle and gives birth to manifestation as the principle of life. Then the actual form of life in the second male principle, the Vau. Then finally the second receptive, female principle, the Hé, when the new life takes tangible shape and from that shape destroys itself to bring forth a further cycle of life.

Thus we start with the first sephira, Kether, the Godhead, which manifests itself in the two pillars and these two are then resolved in the middle column in Daath, the invisible sephira. Daath then begins the new cycle which splits into Chesed and Geburah on the two pillars and this cycle in turn is resolved and destroyed in the middle column in the Sun, which again starts a new cycle lower down the Tree through the two pillars in Netzach and Hod, which are resolved once again in the middle in the sphere of the soul of the Moon before physical form is finally assumed in the sphere of the Earth.

In this way we can see that in the new cycles, the first spark always emanates from the middle, splits on the two pillars and is resolved again in the middle. This fourth aspect of life, or God, which the ancients termed God the Destroyer, is one which lost its meaning when the form of God as a Trinity was adopted and, as Jung has pointed out in his writings, is the main cause of imbalance which led to a sense of alienation and sin in orthodox religion, in our western culture. For the fourth aspect, instead of being regarded as a natural aspect of God's being, fell from grace, and became the Devil which was associated with the physical aspect of life, including the physical body. It is therefore apposite that in therapy the first task, and the most important, is to face this aspect of our being, Satan or Saturn, which in Jungian terminology is the Shadow and which in Freudian is the negative side of the subconscious, and realize that it is as much a part of ourselves as the light side.

Unless we appreciate that everything within the psyche is a part of ourselves, we shall inevitably fail to achieve the wholeness that is the goal of therapy, a point that Jung realized only too well. 'The individual who wishes to have an answer to the problem of evil,' he wrote, 'has need, first and foremost, *of self-knowledge*, that is, the utmost possible knowledge of his own wholeness. He must know relentlessly how much good he can do, and what crimes he is capable of, and must beware of regarding that one as real and the other as illusion. Both are elements within his nature, and both are bound to come to light in him, should he wish – as he ought – to live without self-deception or self-illusion.'[1]

3 *A star above the Sun – the individual planets on the Tree*

There is a star above the sun, that is the highest star: it is nobler than the sun and illumines the sun, and all the light that the sun has, it has from this star.

MEISTER ECKHART[2]

The aim of psychotherapy is to be whole. This state of ideal wholeness or balance has been described in accordance with the symbolism of the Tree of Life. The means to achieve this goal is by experiencing all that is within us – all the parts which constitute this whole. In this section we come to the parts. The parts which are here seen in their balanced state on the Tree while in the next chapter we shall see those same parts of the psyche in accordance with the individual pattern that is the Horoscope.

My thesis in this book, which I believe to be the underlying thesis in therapy, is that the parts only have meaning in relation to the whole. Indeed on their own what we for convenience term separate aspects of ourselves have no real existence. Thus consciousness, of itself, implies unconsciousness. Similarly, the principle of assertiveness that we call Mars implies stability which we call Jupiter, harmony which we call Venus, order which we call Saturn, the Ego which we call the Sun, and every other part of the human psyche which is symbolized by the planets and the sephiroth on the Tree.

There are two practical reasons for looking at the basic energies that constitute the psyche before turning to the Birth Chart. First, because on the Tree we see the underlying principles of these energies in themselves and thus we can understand their inner meanings. And second, because we are able to see the relationship of the apparently separate energies to each other.

Let me take the first point. When we look at the personal Horoscope illustrated in Figure 1.1 we see Mars in Taurus in the 12th House. Here we can see how the principle of Mars operates in that particular psyche. But before we reach that stage we should know what the principle of Mars means in itself. It is here, at this initial stage, that a full understanding of the planetary principles is often lacking and I believe that we can be helped to a very great extent by looking in the first instance at these energies as they appear on the Tree.

For on the Tree we see the principles that are represented by the planets and by the sephiroth in their archetypal form. Here, then, we are in the realm, in Jungian terminology, of the collective unconscious. Here we find the core of the archetypes, which Jung called the 'archetypes as such' to differentiate from the archetypes as they appear in the actual, individual psyche. Here we can perhaps say that they are an idea in the mind of God before they manifest in human shape. Then when they are clothed in material form they can be seen in the Horoscope.

Second, we see the innate relationship of each energy to each other. This is of invaluable help when it comes to looking at an individual Horoscope. The tendency in astrology is to look, for example, at Mars in the 12th House in Taurus, as something effectively separate from the other parts of the Horoscope unless it happens to be in some specific aspect to another factor. But the meaning of that Mars is dependent upon each and every factor in the Horoscope, whether or not there are other factors which aspect it. The Mars energy is itself one element of the Saturn, the Jupiter, the Sun, the Venus, the Mercury elements of the psyche and if we look at this energy on its own we miss the whole point of union and balance and shall inevitably fail to bring about the goal of integration that the psyche seeks.

Before I look at the energies in detail, I should clarify one point. In that the Horoscope represents the individual psyche and the Tree represents the ideal psyche to which this individual psyche attains, the two coincide and much can be learned by looking at the two together. It is, however, important that we look for the meaning of the principles rather than try to draw too close parallels where none exist, or where at best there is only a tenuous correspondence between the principles.

With ten sephiroth on the Tree it is tempting to believe that here is an exact correspondence between the two systems. However, the very fact that the three outer planets have only been discovered in the last two centuries makes it clear that an exact correspondence cannot be maintained. It is natural, and it is convenient, now that the outer planets have been discovered, to seek correspondences with the sephiroth and I shall discuss the validity of so doing, but with bodies in the solar system being continually discovered we shall never be able to force an exact correspondence between the factors in the heavens and the various aspects of life.

This is not something that I believe we should be concerned about. Rather, we should welcome diversity and look for the underlying meaning in the factors as a whole. If we wish to go back to basic principles then we can simply regard the factors as numbers and this applies as much to the planets as to the sephiroth. Then, indeed, the correspondence will be more exact, and at the same time, more abstract. The further we get from the absolute, the nearer to tangible manifestation, the more will differentiation be apparent.

Let us then start with the inner principles. The first sephira, starting at the top of the Tree, is Kether, the Crown, and its number is 1. Before the outer planets were discovered this sephira corresponded with their first sphere, the primum mobile, from where all creation emanated. Here is unity, the absolute, God the

Father, perfection and completeness before life or motion were born. In the words of Meister Eckhart: 'In the Father are the primal images of all creatures.'[3] Here then all is contained in its infinity. With the discovery of the three outer planets, we can assign a correspondence with Neptune, representing the need to be at one with the Godhead, the path towards perfection and complete unity.

Life is duality. When the one breaks into the two, then life moves, the first swirlings of the stillness begin, conflict, opposition, polarity, paradox play with and against each other. Chokmah, number 2, was at first associated with the band of the Zodiac or the Fixed Stars, then with Uranus, the lightning flash or heaven, the primal male, yang principle.

Here was creation itself and in it the created, the individual, each one being born under one of the stars in the constellations. It is significant to note that scientists now believe that life was in all probability created by a lightning flash on the waters, so it appears that the images contained in Uranus and Neptune are appropriate even on a mundane level. In esoteric terms Thomas Vaughn has said, 'God in love with His own beauty frames a glass, to view it by reflection.'[4] The underlying feature of the numbers is brought out again by Meister Eckhart: 'The one is eternity, which maintains itself ever alone and without variation. The two is time, which is changeable and given to multiplication.'[5]

Chokmah, or Uranus, opposes Binah, which corresponds to Saturn, and these together with Kether form the Supernal Triangle where the spirit has its abode. It may be objected, on logical grounds, that Saturn as the last of the old planets should not be on this level and on logical grounds that argument has a great deal of merit. On the other hand Saturn as the planet of death is the very principle that of necessity leads us to the beyond, and paradoxically its very materiality provided the form that Jesus embraced on his spiritual journey.

I mentioned in the last section the three-and four-fold aspects of creation and destruction. Saturn with the 3 closes the pattern within its own form. The principle of destruction and new life is clearest in the invisible sephira that lies under this Supernal Triangle. This sephira is Daath, or Knowledge, which has no number and being invisible no correspondence until it was associated, to my mind appropriately, with Pluto.

Pluto was the invisible god of the underworld, the great and terrible judge who ruled with absolute justice. His is the inexorable law which is tempered neither by mercy nor by severity. In his scales the heart is weighed and no power in heaven or earth can influence his judgment. The nature of this principle has been summed up by Thomas a Kempis: 'Always keep in mind your last end, and how you will stand before the just Judge from whom nothing is hid, who cannot be influenced by bribes and excuses, and who judges with justice.'[6]

Through this gate we, each at our appointed time, must pass. At the end when our time is come and at every moment as each day dies with death. This sephira, as we can clearly see from the diagram of the Tree, lies mid-way from the lower levels to the spiritual level. In a literal sense we have to pass through this ground when we die. But this is also the experience we have to pass through in order to reach any higher understanding. This is the point of breaking through, the point of vision or of ecstasy, the point when we suddenly 'know' that something is true and hence its title of Spiritual Knowledge – knowledge in the absolute sense of complete understanding.

This is what Jesus meant when he told Nicodemus that he must be born again – of the spirit. To live we must die and Pluto is the principle of death and re-birth, the phoenix rising from its own ashes, the resurrection after the descent into hell and the death on the cross. The transformation from man to God, the veil of the temple which was rent in twain when Christ died and was born again in his Father. The symbolism of Pluto is particularly apposite here for in it is contained the circle of the spirit above the semi-circle of the soul and the cross of matter and we can see on the Tree that this symbol mirrors the three sephiroth immediately below it – the spirit of the Sun in Tiphareth over the soul of Yesod or the Moon above the body of the Earth in Malkuth.

This last sephira, Malkuth, again breaks the exact correspondence of planets and the Sun and Moon with the ten sephiroth, but its correspondence is no less important and it should serve as a valuable complement to its devaluation in astrology. The mundane sphere is as much a part of the psyche as any other and corresponds with all important inner, diurnal wheel of the Horoscope, the Angles and the Houses and Elements. This sphere must be experienced if the link between the body and the psyche is to be appreciated.

We shall now look in detail at the seven sephiroth that correspond with the Sun, Moon and five planets which were known to our ancestors. Just as Chokmah, the prime yang or male principle, heads the right-hand pillar, so Binah, which corresponds with Saturn, heads the left-hand pillar and is the prime female or yin principle that exists within each of us. There is a clear paradox here just as there is in the pillars as a whole and to some extent this paradox exists in the nature of Saturn.

Binah is the Great Mother and heads the pillar of Severity. Saturn is usually associated with the father and represents discipline, order, form, structure. Instead of avoiding the paradoxes that are contained in these images we should try to understand the basic principles and moreover, as will be apparent when we get beneath the surface, we should then accept the fact that the principles, as life itself, are paradoxical. It is indeed to a large extent this innate ambivalence that creates the conflicts within the psyche.

Saturn can be equated with Satan, the Devil, or with the Shadow in Jung's terms or the unconscious as a whole which Freud regarded as negative or equally with Freud's view of the Superego, the dictates of conscience that are laid down by the parental figures, theoretically by the father who should be the instrument of discipline. The mythology of Saturn itself has changed radically and that of the Greek equivalent, Kronos, is instructive in this context. Binah, too, as the Great Mother is at once the Virgin Mary, the Mother of Sorrows, and also Isis, whose feast days have been taken over as those of Mary by the Christian Church, and as the ambivalent goddess Kali, protector and devourer of her children.

What at first sight appears to be a paradox between the maternal and the paternal principles, between love and discipline, between the protection of one's offspring and the confinement, even destruction, of these can more readily be seen when we look deeper into the symbolism behind the various guises of Binah and Saturn. We shall then be nearer to understanding why it is that the Great Mother heads the *female* pillar of Severity above Geburah-Mars and Hod-Mercury, and why also Saturn represents at once the paternal principle of order and the gate to consciousness in the form of the Shadow.

Saturn in astrology represents the archetypal father-figure, cold and strict, implying the severity of the pillar at whose head Binah stands, even though originally the god in Rome was one of abundance, of the fruits of the earth which culminated in the feast of Saturnalia, one of drunken revelry whose vestiges remain in our own Christmas. Yet he is the mother, the great receptive principle of the sea, Mara, translated into Maria, the mother of God. However, when we look at the Greek counterpart of Saturn, Kronos, we see the same myth that is contained in Kali. For Kronos was the youngest Titan, child of Ouranos, god of Heaven, who devoured his children, except Zeus, who was saved by his wife-sister, Rhea.

Here there is life and death – the mother who is Saturn. Only by dying can we live. Here is the womb, the form which receives the life force of the individual from Uranus. This seed can only grow, it can only become manifest, within the confines of the boundaries of the Saturnian protectiveness contained in the womb-mother. Without the form of Saturn the life force, the individual nature of the spirit would be spent. The spirit is contained in the physical body, God's being was contained in His only-begotten Son. At any level this is true – whether in the form of human life or in an idea or a work of art which needs some tangible form to give it shape.

The seed needs the ground in which to grow. As the child grows up there needs to be a balance between protectiveness and individuality and to some extent growth is a constant battle between these two opposite principles which are placed at the top of the two pillars of the temple. In alchemy, too, the first stage of the work was the sphere of Saturn, representing lead and the material aspect of the world, including the flesh. So this first stage was 'blackening' or 'mortification' when the flesh was destroyed in the crucifixion, or cross of Saturn, as a prelude to re-birth, and so in dying to the world, spiritual realization was gained.

The next sephira, Chesed, corresponds to Jupiter. It is pertinent to stress at this point that although the correspondences exist between the sephiroth and the planets as the same principles exist in both, the placing of the sephiroth on the Tree exemplifies a different balance than that which is generally accepted in astrology. Thus, whereas in astrology Saturn and Jupiter are seen as a pair, as are Mars and Venus and this is implicit in their visual symbols, on the Tree Saturn opposes Uranus, Mars opposes Jupiter, and Venus opposes Mercury.

With Chesed-Jupiter following Binah-Saturn we can see the relationship as one of emergence and development rather than of direct balance on a horizontal axis. This message also comes out clearly if we look again at alchemical symbolism. In the astrological symbolism we see that Saturn and Jupiter both contain the semi-circle of the soul and the cross of matter of the material world, the difference being that in Saturn the cross stands above the half circle, while the placings are inverted in Jupiter's glyph. So in the second stage of the lesser work the soul raises itself out of the earth in order to develop her power and is thus dissolved out of its coagulation in bodily consciousness.

Chesed is the coherence of the form that is patterned in the triangle of Binah. It is the first tangible form, the cube or the pyramid, and thus it lies below the Supernal Triangle because here for the first time we are on the level of manifestation. So the force, the idea of form, is made solid. Jupiter, therefore, stands four-square upon the earth – the material ruler sitting on his throne, holding majesty and power in his hands.

As the ruler of heaven he is the position of authority who reigns because of what he is rather than what he does. Thus he is being rather than action. His is the position of the power and the glory which is invested in the ruler. So here we have the principle of stability, of law and order, of organization, administration and co-operation, hierarchy and teamwork, togetherness, brotherliness and friendship. Its title of Love and its name of Mercy that it takes from its central position on the pillar of Mercy are derived from this basic sense of co-operation.

Thus the love that is incorporated in this sephira is neither the love of relationships that stems from it and is directly below it, nor is it the love of the mother which it stems from and which is seen in the preceding sephira. Rather it is the higher principle of love that the Greeks appreciated which binds people together in the form of a community or organization based on mutual co-operation, a principle which was the basis of the feudal system where the lord was pledged to defend his men and they in turn were pledged to fight for him in times of trouble.

Here, too, we can see the other side of the coin, for this kind of relationship can become ossified and this of course is what happened in the feudal system. When the principle works positively it can be seen as the natural authority that stems as much from within the personality as the actual position of its holder. Here, then, is wisdom and understanding represented in the divine outpouring of unstinted providence with the benefits that are given both in terms of advice and material possessions. Thus, too, on the Tree it is the plane of the Masters, those souls who choose voluntarily to remain behind on earth to help those in need even though they have reached the stage where they could pass beyond.

Just as Jupiter builds up, so Mars breaks down and is directly opposed to it. And here we can see how it is that these two principles need to be directly balanced both in our society and in personal terms within the individual psyche. Jupiter, as I have stated, is. It obtains its authority from its position. Mars acts. It gains its victories from its actions, from what it does, and of course the latter should reflect the former. This is apparent in the images of the two sephiroth. Whereas Chesed sits serenely on his throne, Geburah is the mighty warrior in his chariot.

And Chesed, as the number 4, is the balanced square – stability. Geburah, the 5, is unbalanced, eccentric; it comes to life and moves. From the stability of the four Elements a quintessence is introduced which provides a new direction, unique, individual – Man himself. And so in astrology we have Mars as the motive force, the drive to assert the Ego, to act, to strive, to express that which is within us.

Society has quite naturally stressed the virtues of love and mercy rather than aggression. The result of this emphasis is that the Jupiter principle has been stressed at the expense of the Mars need. What the symbolism of the Tree achieves so well is to state graphically that both principles are necessary aspects of all life and of every human being and that they must balance each other. Although it might in theory be obvious in astrology, in practice without this visual symbolism the point rarely appears to be realized. The blatant emphasis on one side at the expense of the other can be seen in the title of Jupiter as the Great Benefic and Mars as the Lesser Malefic, but even today Jupiter is too often assumed to be only the provider of bounty and good fortune while Mars is at best regarded with suspicion as a necessary evil.

The result of this is that the natural outgoing Mars force is driven underground, often with disastrous effects for the individual concerned and we shall examine this situation in greater detail later in this book when we deal with the planetary energies more specifically. In the wider social context it is necessary both to build up stable forms and to break down these forms so that evolution can take place. On a personal as well as a social level there should be a continuing cycle of growth and destruction and renewed growth if life is to go on. In practice there is always a tendency, once an organization has been built up from its initial vision to settle down and grow stagnant until a new force comes to give life to the old form, or alternatively to break up the old form completely and set up a new one.

On the principle of equilibrium, the greater the emphasis on one side, the greater will be the pressure on the other side to swing the pendulum towards balance. Thus the more something has been built up, the more stable it has become, the greater the degree of destruction will be necessary to bring about change. In personal terms we have kindness, love and mercy on one side and discipline and severity on the other. While kindness and growth are virtues in themselves, too much emphasis on these principles is as harmful as excess in the opposite direction. As Martin Luther King said: 'We will have to repent, in this generation, not so much for the evil deeds of wicked people, but for the appalling silence of the good people.' So growth turns to cancer and the knife is necessary. It turns to fat and exercise is necessary. It turns to economic over-expansion which needs to be checked.

Geburah-Mars acts as the corrector of balance by drastic means, the cutting of the Gordian knot, the surgeon with his knife. The declaration of war to protect the weak, Christ throwing the money-changers out of the temple, the courage to stand up against the majority for one's beliefs. It is the outgoing energy, the pioneering spirit, the impetus to discover, to initiate, to dare, to assert oneself, to become an individual. So it is the means to justice which, if taken too far, can lead to cruelty, tyranny and destruction. As such it is the executive arm of justice rather than the principle of justice itself which, as we have seen, is the sphere of Daath or Pluto – the absolute truth and the law, not one iota of which shall be taken away. Mars is the sword that enforces this justice while Jupiter is the authority and the organization behind it. And to emphasize that there are no irrevocable laws the absolute principle of Daath or Pluto is tempered with mercy and severity according to specific circumstances.

The individuality of Geburah-Mars itself needs to be resolved in a balanced way. The five-pointed star, the pentacle of Magic, changes into the six-pointed star of David where there is perfect harmony. This ideal state, that of Beauty which is the name assigned to Tiphareth, sums up the goal and the path of the whole Tree. Here is our centre, our heart. This is the abode of the Sun, Apollo, who was the god of healing, and as Malachi states: 'But onto you that fear my name shall the Sun of righteousness arise with healing in his wings.'[7]

In Jungian terminology Tiphareth or the Sun represents the Ego, the centre of consciousness. When we are centred, when we find our Christ-centre, then we can get in touch with the Self which is represented by the Tree as a whole and the Birth Chart as a whole. Once again the visual symbol of the Tree illustrates so well this central force. It also helps to explain the nature of the spirit in relation to the soul and the physical body and indeed to God in a way the Horoscope does not. According to the astrological symbolism spirit, soul and body are symbolized by the circle, the semi-circle and the cross respectively. This is valid so far as it goes but it does not show how these principles manifest in relation to each other or to the rest of one's being.

For this reason there is often confusion as to whether the spirit is contained in the Birth Chart and this is because no differentiation is made between the spirit and God. We can regard God as the spirit of the whole of life and the essence of this principle is contained in Kether, in our desire or need to be a part of a greater whole. It was this need that Jung stated to be an integral part of the human psyche, rejecting Freud's material view that it represented only physical sublimation.

What we call the spirit, however, is our own centre. The essence of oneness and unity that has been planted in our psyches as the circle of the spirit has been impregnated with the seed-dot in its centre. This is as far as we can get in this incarnation as again is made clear by the placing of Tiphareth below Daath and the Supernal Triangle. This image of God which we call the spirit is reflected in what we call the soul, which once again lies directly under Tiphareth in the form of Yesod on the Tree.

From this central point the unity of the spirit or the Ego is split up and we arrive at the senses – the two sides of the brain: rational and intuitive, through which everything must pass in order that it can be assimilated. So here we have the intuition of Netzach and the rational, perspective of Hod, or art and science. Netzach-Venus, as the number 7, represents the seven colours of the rainbow which are derived from the unity of the Sun's rays and God's love for His people made manifest, both in the symbol of Venus which incorporates the circle of the Sun-spirit over the physical cross of matter, and also in the rainbow which was God's covenant and promise to His people – again uniting the God of Heaven or the sky with His children on Earth.

The pure beauty of symmetry which we saw in the Sun is now brought into the world – through human relationships, the love of one person for another, and the love of beauty on earth and the love of the earth itself through the feelings and emotions – the joy of creativity and living. And whereas through Netzach-Venus we feel, in Hod-Mercury we think, observe through the concrete mind in mental images and rational thought processes and learn to communicate.

So the force of Netzach, the creative inspiration, is put into concrete form in mental concepts, into writing or speech in Hod. Here, too, we can see the same underlying principles running down the pillars from their essence to concrete forms of expression. Just as the creative force of life is given form by the Great Mother, Saturn, and substance through the power of the mind in Hod, so the creative power of Chokmah-Uranus finds tangible expression in the senses of Netzach. It may also be said that to understand astrology both aspects of the mind, the intuitive and the rational, must be used. Then we shall acquire the wisdom and understanding that lie at the summit of the pillars and appreciate that astrology is both a science and an art.

These two principles are resolved in Yesod which corresponds to the Moon. This is the way we react both to the world around us through the mind and the senses of the two previous sephiroth and also to the spirit above. And the way we react is of the utmost importance. There has been an unfortunate tendency to devalue the importance of this factor, especially in astrology. It should always be borne in mind that the Sun and Moon are equal partners, the two primal yang-yin energies which manifest in the pillars themselves.

Jung certainly made this clear and even tried to some extent to redress the balance after Freud by suggesting that, as consciousness evolved from the unconscious, if anything it was the unconscious side which was the more important. Certainly it is here, according to his views, that the real needs of each one of us resides. Thus, in the words of Whitmont: 'The course of therapy that follows Jung's approach is based on a continuous dialogue between the conscious ego and the unconscious.'[8] Whether we accept the views of Freud or Jung in believing that the unconscious is positive or negative, it cannot be denied that great power resides in the unconscious and that it is only by bringing out this power that our troubled psyches can be healed and the life force positively redirected.

The spirit of the Sun must be received in the soul of the Moon. In order to achieve this state we need to be open. When we listen to the voice within, when we are truly receptive through the power of the Moon principle then, and then alone, can we receive the spirit and learn the truth. Then the spirit can dwell finally in our human bodies in Malkuth and then the two sides of our psyches become united.

CHAPTER 4

The Horoscope – the model of the individual Psyche

All that God ever created is nothing but an image and a sign of eternal life.

MEISTER ECKHART[1]

In the last chapter we saw the Tree of Life as the model of the ideal psyche. In this chapter we shall look at the same energies as they are arranged in the Horoscope. Just as the Tree enables us to see the psyche in its ideal state both as a whole and as a number of separate energies, so the Horoscope enables us to see both the whole and the separate aspects of the individual psyche. When we combine the two we learn to see in the fifth dimension and perceive the spirit.

We start with unity and we end with unity. The psyche is a living organism which begins in a state of unconscious wholeness. At this stage the child is in the womb or so attached to its mother that its solipsistic viewpoint is undifferentiated. Here there is the Horoscope as a whole, the unbroken wheel of the Birth Chart which contains the seed of its innate potential. From then on, in the words of Anthony Storr: 'Normal development is characterised by a process whereby progressive differentiation of the object is accompanied by a progressive decrease in identification.'[2] From the primordial unity, duality is developed. The Ego breaks away from the unconscious as the child strives to assert itself as an independent being. The Sun-Moon polarity divides into two with the differentiated male-female or yang-yin energies.

In the beginning there is only the One – the Horoscope as a

whole pattern or the Sun-Moon syzygy. Then the One breaks down into the Two – the Sun and Moon are severed from each other and form the opposing sides of the psyche, the conscious and unconscious, the masculine and the feminine. From the Sun and Moon all the other factors in turn develop just as the development of the child is dependent on the way he perceives the original parental images. If we see the factors in the Horoscope, the Sun, Moon, planets and Angles, in this way we no longer see them as separate entities but as a gradual process of evolution from unity to multiplicity. In Figure 4.1, I have tried to convey this concept of inherent evolution in a visual form.

The Ascendant then becomes the way that the child perceives the Sun-Moon image, Saturn that which he rejects in that image, Mars the way he directs his solar energy, Venus the way he comes to terms with his lunar energy. In the same way all the factors in the Horoscope are in essence derivatives of the primal Sun-Moon polarity which itself is the division of the Horoscope into its dual aspect. Thus the Ascendant in Figure 1.1 is not an isolated entity which is unconnected with the rest of Rosalind's Birth Chart. Viewed like this we can see that she has her Ascendant in Taurus and her Saturn in Leo in accordance with her perception of the parental images described by the positions of her Sun and Moon.

Equally, we can see that each separate factor is in itself a whole and contains within itself its own space-time continuum. These factors are images that describe the inner world of the individual but inasmuch as the world outside is viewed in accordance with the images themselves the one will inevitably be reflected in the other. It is this inner world that the therapist tries to see through his relationship with the individual and which the astrologer can see directly in the symbolism of the Horoscope. Anthony Storr makes the point in this passage:

It would, of course, be argued that, ultimately, symbolic solutions are the only appropriate answer to severe emotional problems. Most difficulties in interpersonal

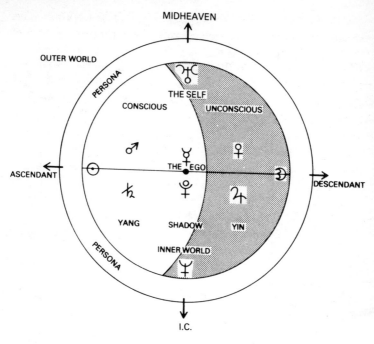

Figure 4.1 *The Horoscope in its natural state*

relationships ... are actually referable to the 'inner worlds' of the persons concerned and not to the actual personalities of the world of reality. It is the images from this inner world which are projected upon other people which cause the trouble, and it is coming to terms with these images, or finding some way of dealing with them which is the principal task of any kind of analysis.'[3]

The images are originally brought into being in accordance with the influence of the parents or other significant people, but it is not those influences, as objective circumstances, that can be seen in the Horoscope. What can be seen is the way the individual perceives, on an unconscious level, such influences or people. Thus it is not the mother in any objective sense that is described by the Moon in the Horoscope but the individual's view of the mother. The corollary is that the individual's feelings, her instinctive reactions, her own feminine side are the direct result of the way she perceives the maternal principle and it is this image which is described by the Moon in her Horoscope.

By seeing the reality of these images in their own perspective the astrologer as therapist can enable the individual to experience them for himself in their entirety. He can see how the images originated, how they manifest in the present and how they can be transformed in the future. In this way he enables the individual to come to terms with the various aspects of his nature and by seeing also how they are derived from the same source he brings about the ultimate union with that source.

1 *The sun-moon polarity – conscious and unconscious*
    Man does, woman is.

                                        EDWARD EDINGER

The Sun and Moon symbolize the two poles of the psyche, the opposing active and receptive, or yang-yin energies which are represented on the Tree of Life in their synthesizing role in the middle column and then as the two pillars themselves which in their differentiated state contain the planetary energies. In this section I shall look at the Sun and Moon in their primary form, as energies in themselves, and then later in the chapter we shall see how they contain the seeds of their opposites, as the anima and animus.

As symbols of the present, the Sun represents the individual's inner power, his active, assertive, masculine, yang side; while the Moon represents the receptive nature, the intuitive power, the immediate and instinctive attunement to others and to the world outside, the feminine, feeling, yin side. As the aim of the psyche is harmony there should be a balance between these two sides, so that doing reflects being. So by being consciously in touch with the unconscious, a person acts in accordance with his nature as a whole and he attains integrity.

Although the Sun represents consciousness while the Moon represents the unconscious a person will not necessarily be in touch with his Sun or out of touch with his Moon. Indeed, because the Moon represents a person's more immediate, instinctive nature it is often the side that he will appear to be more in touch with and certainly the aspect of his nature which is more apparent to others. We should therefore regard the Sun as symbolizing the potential for conscious awareness, in Jungian terminology as the Ego, the means of integrating the various factors in the Horoscope into a whole, or into the Self, the hero in his quest to reach the Grail.

The Moon, on the other hand, represents our deepest needs, the foundations of which have been laid down unconsciously. How far the individual is in touch with either side is something that can be seen from the positions of the Sun and Moon themselves in the context of the Horoscope as a whole. When we look at these bodies as symbols of the past, we see the original influences that moulded the images which will normally be the parents. It is therefore important to appreciate just what can be seen in these images so far as they relate to the parents.

Here we meet the basic divergence concerning the parental influences according to the different schools of psychology. This divergence is particularly apparent when the 'object-relations' school of analysts who base their views on those of Freud is compared with the Jungian school. The Freudians see the psyche as a blank screen, upon which the parents apply their influence, although the images which are produced by these influences are not necessarily in accordance with the actual behaviour of the parents.

Certainly Freud saw the character purely as a result of outside influences. What the 'object-relations' school refer to as 'internal objects' represent the images of the parents and other significant figures and these are derived from the infant's earliest experiences. These are 'introjected' within the psyche and influence all the child's subsequent experience of actual people in the external world. The result has been described by Eric Berne: 'When the individual grows up his parents are not usually standing beside him to punish him if he does not do as they think he ought, but their powerful and heavily charged images are there in his mind.'[4]

The Jungian view, in theory at any rate, is that these images are derived from an inborn disposition. In the words of Whitmont: 'There is a realm of predetermined personality potentials ... which are not merely products of the environment, though environmental factors may succeed in evoking them.'[5] Jung believed that there are certain archetypal principles, or cores, which are common to everyone and which thus lie beyond the personal, in what he termed the 'collective unconscious'. These archetypes are part of our common heritage which are symbolized in myth in every culture. The mother will always be the Mother, or Demeter or Kali. The archetypes are then moulded into specific images depending on the actual upbringing and the individual's own peculiar pattern or disposition. In this way we can see what Jung called the 'archetypes as such' in the sephiroth on the Tree, and the specific images which are moulded around these archetypal cores in the individual Horoscope.

Thus the archetypal father is, in the words of Storr: 'the representation of the spirit whose function is to oppose pure instinctuality.'[6] Here we see the Sun opposing the Moon. When, however, we look more closely at these viewpoints, it becomes apparent that the divergence is not so marked as may at first sight appear. It is clear that the child is influenced by the parents, and indeed by others who are close to him during the early period of his development. Although Freud was more concerned with the real parents, or other significant people, and eschewed the term 'archetype' as a general, cultural force, nonetheless it is not the actual parents who leave their mark but the way that the child views those parents, and inevitably all fathers and all mothers will act in much the same way. Whether we call this general way of acting, of being a mother or a father, the principle or archetype of 'motherhood' or 'fatherhood' and endow it with a generic or god name, is to a large degree a matter of description and emphasis.

Jungian psychologists appreciate that the only way to see the archetypal parents is through the actual parental images. In other words they can only deal with the mythological core in personal terms. As Whitmont writes:

> Only when the personal (the ontogenetic) is fully explained can the archetypal core of the complex effectively be reached, because the personal shell of the complex is the form in which the external mythological motif incarnates itself and makes itself felt in our personal life and our personal nature.[7]

In this way we can see that not only are the primal active and receptive energies embodied in the parental images, but that these in turn develop into the means to deal with those energies in specific ways through Mars and Venus, which are thus directly derived from the Sun and Moon respectively. To quote Whitmont again: 'Inasmuch as ordering activity and emotional receptivity are felt as belonging to the masculine and feminine principles respectively, the first life contacts with father and mother set the basic patterns for the development of our assertiveness and feeling.'[8]

Let us now look at the Sun and Moon in the Birth Chart with these viewpoints in mind. It should be clear from the very fact that what we are looking at is a *Birth* Chart that no actual influence occurring after the birth can have the slightest effect on any factor in that Chart. The Birth Chart itself does not change no matter what the parents or anyone else do, and no matter what views the individual forms of any outside influence. But this in itself merely has the effect of shifting the situation one stage back. When we look at what happens in practice it is clear that the way

the child interacts with the parents and others does describe
aspects of their relationship. However, the Birth Chart itself is the
result of the parents who created it. Thus the temperament, or
inborn disposition, of the child is itself a result of the parental
influences and in reality the two cannot be separated.

My view is that what can be seen in the Birth Chart in the
symbols of the Sun and Moon is the way the individual views, on a
subjective and unconscious level, his parents or other significant
people. The planets represent, according to Jungian terminology,
archetypal cores and thus there will always be a principle of
motherhood and fatherhood whether or not there was a real
mother or father, and whichever role any particular parent took
in reality. So it is that Saturn, which is traditionally symbolic of
the father, will sometimes reflect the maternal influence rather
than that of the father, and why on occasion it will reflect aspects
of both parents. Also, because the Sun and Moon are a pair, the
way one parent is perceived will inevitably affect the individual's
perception of the other. Thus a mother who is stronger, or merely
closer, than a father may be viewed as dominating and the father
weak according to the positions of Sun and Moon even though, in
reality, neither parent were anything but normal.

What then is the purpose of looking at these factors in terms of
parental images? Once again we can see a basic divergence of
viewpoint in those who adhere to the different schools. I shall look
at these viewpoints shortly. At this stage it needs to be born in
mind that the Birth Chart is the pattern of the individual
throughout his life and that to understand a person as a whole, the
present needs to be seen in the context of both the past and the
future. In that the images which are symbolized by the Sun and
Moon are laid down in the unconscious they will continue to
affect the individual throughout his life. The woman with Sun
square Neptune may consciously regard her father as the perfect,
ideal embodiment of manhood but unconsciously regard him as
weak and ineffective. In the present, with this complex referring
to her own active, assertive side she may set herself what she

believes to be realistic goals but unconsciously ensure that she fails to meet them. In the future she may attract on an unconscious level men who appear to be strong and capable, but who in some way turn out to be ineffectual or impotent.

Thus the purpose is not to cast blame on the parents or on anyone else, but to try to help the individual to understand himself and his complexes. The point is for the therapist to be aware of the total situation whether or not the influences are actually relevant at the time he is treating the patient. By making the patient aware of the significance of his complexes through the factors in his Birth Chart, by making him conscious of them, he is able to experience the energies and use them for himself. Those complexes, as aspects of his Horoscope, remain with him and are a part of him. Only by experiencing them in their totality can he integrate them and transform them within himself.

One should, of course, be concerned with the present and in many ways the emphasis away from the past that we have seen in the Humanist-Existential schools is a good thing. But the real point is to be free from the past, and that goal is not achieved by avoiding the past or pretending that it does not exist. Like any other part of one's total being, whether in space or time, the past can only be integrated if the individual has succeeded in reconciling it, and this often means that he has to go back to the past and exorcise it before he is able to live in the present.

Freud's view was that people became stuck in the present and that their regression to past fixations was derived from a block in the past. This occurred because they had never succeeded in solving the past. The past then became repressed into the unconscious and the individual constantly met it in the present. It is certainly an over-simplification to say that Freud was concerned only with the past, while Jung and his followers were concerned with the present alone. While there is an element of truth in this assertion, the reason is that the two dealt mainly with different kinds of patients. Freud's patients, as we have seen, were mostly in the first half of life when they were concerned with problems of

relating and activity, while Jung's patients had in the main passed
that point and were concerned with the question of inner meaning
and life's purpose.

When Jung did deal with patients who suffered from more
outward problems then he too would look at the past, as Jacobi
makes clear: '(then) an analysis of the repressed "ontogentic"
contents ... is sufficient. They correspond roughly to the
problems of childhood and youth considered by Freud, and for this
reason Jung too, in such cases, would take account of the Freudian
viewpoints, though giving them rather a different accent.'⁹ The
aim, then, is to meet the factors in the Horoscope in order to
understand them in their entirety. The parental influences affect
and mould unconsciously the way the individual behaves in the
present. If we accept the past, if necessary we exorcise it, then we
can gain the power to transform it and ourselves into a creative
present with which we can meet the future which is our destiny.
In this way we can take the first step towards wholeness or
integration.

2 *From darkness to light – the Ego, the Shadow and the Persona*
   Life itself is but the shadow of death ... the Sun itself is but the
   dark simulacrum, and light but the shadow of God.
                                            SIR THOMAS BROWNE

When the primal unity divides the world of paradox is born. From
the undifferentiated whole the opposites form. Each aspect of the
psyche throws up a reflection, a dark unconscious side that mirrors
the conscious. Before we can be conscious of the whole that is the
Self, we need to be divided to so that we can see ourselves. Even
God had to create man in order to see His own nature.

We have seen the first division – from the unconscious total
identification with the mother into the gradual awakening of
consciousness as the child begins to separate himself and evolves
into a person in his own right. So the Ego, the assertive side of the
psyche, the potential for individuation, symbolized by the Sun,

tries to break away from its womb-source and oppose the pure instinctuality of the Moon. Thus the Ego, the Sun, is the centre of consciousness – the Christ-centre, the healing god Apollo residing in the centre of the Tree of Life, and in the Horoscope a miniature whole, the same circle revolving around its hub that is the Horoscope itself.

The Ego then is the path to individuality or individuation. It is the means whereby we can consciously unite with the unconscious. But, as I have pointed out in the last section, this conscious side, or Sun centre, is not necessarily the part that we are most in touch with. Indeed, just as we cannot look directly at the Sun, so we cannot reach the symbolic Sun directly. How then do we get in touch with the Sun? Just as the Horoscope splits into the Sun-Moon polarity, so the Sun itself splits into two polar opposites, the Ego breaks down into the Shadow and the Persona.

As the child needs to be accepted by his parents, those parts of the Self which do not meet acceptance, or which the child believes will not be accepted by his parents, become repressed. This dark, unacceptable side is the Shadow. Those parts which are acceptable, or which the child believes will be accepted by his parents, become the Persona. Thus the Persona is the aspect of the psyche to which one relates most consciously. In the words of Jolande Jacobi: 'One could say with a little exaggeration, that the persona is that which in reality one is not, but which oneself as well as others think one is.'[10]

And the same therapist has described the Shadow as: 'the sum of all the qualities conforming to our sex that were neglected or rejected while the ego was being built up.'[11] Thus there is an innate compensatory relationship between these opposing aspects of the psyche. The more a person identifies with his role, the more he is concerned with the way he appears to others and comes over to them, the less in touch with his true individuality will he be, and the more negative and darker will be his real personality. Conversely, the greater his anxiety about his darker side, the more he is concerned about his Shadow, the more defensive will he appear to others, and the more negative will his Persona become.

The Shadow is symbolized by Saturn, the dark angel or Satan, and here we see that which we fear and that which we repress with the greatest emotional intensity, that is, those things which we project and dislike the most in others because we cannot bear to accept them as parts of our own nature. The Persona, on the other hand, is represented in its clearest form by the Ascendant, although I believe that it is best seen as the diurnal circle as a whole which is focused in its most personal aspect in the Rising point. This is the way we project ourselves in the world to others and the way we like to be seen and accepted and thus the way we tend to see ourselves.

I quoted Dr Jacobi who defined the Persona as 'that which in reality one is not' but we should be careful of accepting this statement literally. Very often the Persona is regarded as something false or unreal, as no more than a mask which should be dispensed with in order to reach one's true being which is contained in the Sun alone. Of course the term 'persona' in its literal sense is the mask that the Greek actors wore on stage and there is an element of truth in regarding this as a false front.

Nevertheless the temptation to regard this aspect of the psyche as something that is false should be avoided. If we accept the thesis that psychic healing is a matter of becoming whole by experiencing and getting in touch with everything in the psyche, and thus with each part of the Horoscope, then we must accept that every part is as valid and real, and indeed necessary, as every other part. Certainly we need to reach the Ego – that is the way to integrate the psyche as a whole and thus to find the Self. But the way to reach the Ego is through the Shadow and the Persona. The latter is the most easily accessible, while the former is the least.

The Persona can then be seen as the expression of the archetypal drive towards an adaptation to external reality and collectivity. We live among other people, we exist in a social context and we need to take other people into account. At the same time we need to be true to ourselves. If we do only what we believe others will find acceptable or what we believe they expect of us, we inevitably make people uncomfortable because they recognize that we are being false as individuals.

The Persona should express the ego and we should thus attain the inner confidence to relate to others through the Persona. The point, therefore, is that the Persona should be flexible. Sometimes a person associates with his role in the world to the extent that it is virtually impossible to get through to him, and equally impossible for him to get through to others. Here the mask has become too rigid and this can be seen, for example, when a person assumes the role of a particular profession, like the priest or policeman who cannot act as a real human being even to his own family. At the other extreme there are people with Personas that are so underdeveloped that their transparency is embarrassing.

In Figure 4.2, Pauline has a Libran Ascendant. She was made to believe that everything had to be beautiful and harmonious. Provided she did everything in the right way, provided she ensured that all was tasteful and pleasant on the surface, she would be accepted. Saturn, on the other hand, symbolizes that which she had been taught was unacceptable. With that factor in Scorpio, the real, deeply held emotions were wrong and were therefore repressed and so she felt unable to express her deep feelings. Here fear held sway with emotional intensity and she came to associate the expression of naked feelings with distaste if not revulsion.

One can see from this example how these two polar opposites affect an individual paradoxically. The person who is afraid to express his real feelings, who is neat and tidy on the outside, who believes that he must do what others expect of him, that it is not 'nice' to talk about sex, yet alone be involved in physical proximity with another person, inevitably represses his vital life-force which needs some outlet. He may even end up in extreme form like the character in John Fowles's *The Collector* who is so dead to his real feelings that he attracts all that is beautiful only in the form of death.

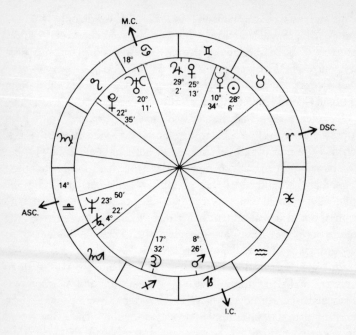

Figure 4.2   *Horoscope of Pauline*

Pauline needs to be in touch with her Taurean Sun, but as she
has a Libran Ascendant what she must do, and can only do, is to
get in touch with her Taurean Sun through her Libran Ascendant.
The aim then is to balance the opposing forces so that the light of
the Sun can shine through the Rising point. If the Persona is too
strong then it will prevent this vital access. And it can be too
strong either because it is too bright or because it is too dark. An
unintegrated Scorpio Ascendant can block out the light of a Leo
Sun, for example. One might sense that there is an outgoing,
creative inner self which is unable to emerge. But the reverse is as
often true. The sensitivity of a Cancerian Sun can be as
defensively hidden by a Leo Ascendant which blinds the inner

light by pride or arrogance. This person may appear at first sight to be outgoing and confident but the real feelings cannot be expressed any more than the inner spirit can with the individual who has a Leo Sun. In neither case is the person being true to himself.

Thus the Persona is the aspect of the psyche with which one is most in touch. The Shadow, on the other hand, is the part with which one is least in touch and just as the aim of therapy in general is to enable the individual to get in touch with his unconscious side, so the way to reach the Ego along the path of the Persona-Shadow axis is through the unconscious side of this pair. Whitmont has made the point that: 'No progress or growth in analysis is possible until the shadow is adequately confronted.'[12] Much of the early stages of analysis are taken up in the attempt to discover the nature of this Shadow area in the psyche. And much of the subsequent process of analysis is taken up in getting the patient to experience this area for himself.

Just as the Persona needs to be accepted and faced so that it can be transformed, so does the Shadow. Then the lead of Saturn can be turned into the gold of the Sun. In the words of Jacobi: 'To confront a person with his shadow is to show him his own light.'[13] This is Satan as Lucifer, the light-bearer. When we face this shadow we see that its form stretches over us and forms the protecting hands of God who blesses us with His Love. There we find the gate which leads the hero towards his Grail.

3 *When the sun breaks down – the anima and animus*

All women become like their mothers. That is their tragedy. No man does. That's his.

OSCAR WILDE, *The Importance of Being Earnest*

We have seen that the Sun and Moon represent the two sides of the human psyche – the yang-yin forces which constantly oppose each other and which need to be balanced. The way to resolve the opposites, as always, is to experience the other side which resides within each of them. We shall now look at the Sun and Moon in terms of the animus and anima, whereby the male has the seed of the female within his psyche through his anima, and the female has the male seed within her psyche through her animus. The need for balance can be seen in both the western model of the ideal psyche, the Tree of Life, where the yang and yin pillars lie on either side of the central column of equilibrium which itself contains both the Sun and the Moon, and also in the eastern model of the Tao, where the two halves of the circle each contain the seed of the other.

Thus the man needs to experience his feminine 'other half' and the woman her masculine 'other half'. The way these aspects of the psyche are formed through the original parental images is made clear in this passage by Whitmont:

> By the law of association, whatever experiences correspond to or are contiguous to the way the Feminine was first and most impressively met form a pattern of *a priori* expectations which continue to function throughout the individual's life. This will colour not only his relationships with particular women but also his emotions, fastases and imaginings ... In other words, the complexes formed around the anima core direct the man's reactions to emotional situations and to particular women and also shape his unconscious expectations of the way they will behave.[14]

And by the same law of association, the woman's experiences of the male govern her image of men and her own assertiveness.

Here we can see how the image of the father-figure is transformed into the animus for women, the archetypal male or yang force which is a fixed constant within a woman's psyche. In general terms it represents her potential for being herself, the source of her own power or individuality, her assertive nature in its primal form. In specific terms it is the image of men that is within her and which she will then project onto the men whom she attracts in her life. And in the same way the image of the mother-figure becomes the anima for men which represents both a man's emotional and feeling side in general and his image of women in particular.

We have seen how the animus and anima originate through the parental images and how they are transformed into aspects of the psyche of the individual. When we turn to the question of how the individual is to experience his anima or her animus, we are faced again with the controversy between those therapists who stress the outer world of activity and relationships and those who emphasize inner meaning and values. Anthony Storr in his biography of Jung naturally stresses the latter approach through the 'inner worlds' in the passage I quoted above.

Others, however, would argue that, although the images are present in the 'inner world' of the individual, that in itself does not necessarily mean that the resolution of the problems also lies within the psyche. Indeed Storr himself, in the same work, makes the point that the emphasis by Jung on these inner worlds, indeed his whole concept of the anima and animus, was derived from the fact that he was himself an emotionally isolated child. And to a great extent the emphasis of one school of therapy will depend on the temperaments of those who adhere to that particular school.

It should also be appreciated that the divergence between the two views is partly a matter of emphasis. Although Jung was more interested in the interior world of his patients, inevitably because of his own temperament, he did not feel that relationships were unimportant. He was personally more concerned with people who had solved the problems of the outer world and were entering the second half of their lives and so had different needs – specifically the need to find meaning within themselves.

The conclusion that the individual needs to form a relationship between the two sides of his own psyche is common ground. What matters in a particular instance is how this relationship can best be brought about. In some way the woman needs to express her assertive side, her yang energies. In some way, the man needs to express his feelings, his yin energies. If these energies are repressed, if they remain in the unconscious, then they will be projected onto the world outside, onto the members of the opposite sex whom the individual attracts and onto the events that he or she also attracts.

It is sometimes suggested that projection is a negative way of dealing with a problem area. In reality it is not only a natural phenomenon but virtually the only means of bringing the problem out into the open so that the inner worlds can be seen. The therapist himself reflects these inner worlds through the relationship between himself and the patient whereby the problem areas are projected onto him.

Projection in itself will not of course solve the problem. If the part which is projected is unacceptable to the individual, as is usually the case, then he will simply blame the person on whom his anima has been projected. If, on the other hand, he can see his anima reflected in his partner, then he can attempt to experience his problem areas through the relationship which is formed as the result of his projection. In some form the repressed side, the anima or animus which is within the unconscious, needs to be expressed and experienced. The Sun should represent the woman's own Ego and not simply her 'other half' in the sense of a husband. If she merely ends up living through her partner then the whole point is missed. In the same way a man should be helped to experience his own feelings through his relationship with a woman and thus integrate his Moon within himself.

So long as the man's anima and the woman's animus are experienced it does not matter how the relationship is affected. Having said that, and accepting that not everyone wants or needs to form a relationship with another person, it must be admitted that it is certainly more difficult to form a relationship internally and there can be a real danger that in avoiding a relationship with another person the other side is never fully integrated. This, of course, is why Freud stressed the importance of personal relationships, and why Jung did not advocate avoiding them but rather emphasized the need for some people to develop a meaningful relationship within themselves once they had passed the stage of relationships in the outer world. Even St Paul, hardly a great lover of women, recognized that 'he who loveth his wife loveth himself.'

There is a real need to develop inwardly and to fill the existential void that exists within the psyche. But there can also be the temptation to go in before the problems of the world in the first half of life have been solved. One's other half can certainly be found through art, social work or spiritual illumination. A woman can find her masculine half through pioneering or embracing a cause and a man his feminine half through poetry or spiritual endeavours. At the same time it is, I think, a great mistake to turn to alternative ways of understanding before the individual is ready to do so, and in particular as an avoidance of human relationships and living in the world. The aim is not to cut oneself off from the world but to find the spirit in the world. Heaven and earth are two sides of the same reality and each is as important as the other. Meaning, as an expression of the whole Self, should not be an avoidance but a consummation.

4 *Personal values and differentiation*

From the basic principles of yang and yin symbolized by the Sun and Moon we now come to differentiation within these principles. The Ego, or source of our inner power, symbolized by the Sun, is broken down into Mars, as the drive to assert that power, the motive force which enables the solar energy to be accomplished; and Saturn, as the framework or form within which that drive can function in the material world. Equally, the receptive, emotional power of the Moon produces the means of expressing our feelings through relationships and harmony in Venus; and within the greater love for humanity which is encompassed in the protectiveness and faith of Jupiter.

If we look at the planets in this way, as the means to achieve the goal of the psyche and bring about the reconciliation of the two primal yang-yin forces, then we can see how the individual factors in the Horoscope, although expressing principles of their own, are also part of the Horoscope as a whole. Then there will be less temptation to split up the whole by regarding the planetary energies as sub-personalities, a view which has been encouraged by certain schools of psychology.

Each planet symbolizes an archetypal energy that is present in the human psyche as it is present in life as a whole. Thus Mars symbolizes the force of assertiveness, aggressiveness, anger and forcefulness. But if we look at this energy in isolation we will not succeed in resolving the psyche into the unique pattern it is. We shall neither be able to see whence this energy came nor how it fits into the total complex that is the Horoscope. That is why it is essential that we recognize the planetary energies as direct derivatives of the two primal energies. Then we shall no longer look upon Mars as separate from the rest of the Birth Chart, but being formed as a direct result of the Sun's position and as the instrument of the solar force.

The archetypal interconnectedness of each apparently separate factor in the Horoscope, the several planetary energies including the Sun and Moon, is contained in their ideal state in the model of that Tree of Life. It was for that reason that I began by looking at that model in the last chapter before turning to these energies in the specific context of the individual psyche in the Horoscope in this chapter. In the model of the Tree we can see quite clearly that each planetary energy, which in its fundamental form is a number, is derived from the preceding numbers. Here, too, we saw the way in which these energies are balanced in their ideal state.

The position of Saturn is paradoxical because although it represents the aspect of the yang force that provides structure and form, it is associated with the Great Mother on the Tree. Saturn was traditionally regarded as the ruler of the Sun by the ancients and the paradox is apparent when we consider that although the Shadow opposes the Ego which is symbolized by the Sun, nonetheless Saturn leads us to the unconscious which is symbolized by the Moon. Thus the gate of heaven is contained in the earth and we can only ascend towards our spiritual nature by living in the world and then dying in the flesh. So at the lowest point, at the nadir, the opposites are resolved.

Jupiter, too, is paradoxical and is, I believe, the most misunderstood planet of all. Traditionally this factor is regarded as a male force through its association with the King of the gods, even though both Saturn and Uranus ruled in heaven before they were in turn supplanted by their youngest offspring, and as the provider of good fortune, even though the gifts of Jupiter were as destructive in Roman myth as are many of the mundane aspects of his force today. At the same time he is also associated with the principle of greater harmony and the love of humanity as a co-operative body before it is personalized through relationships in Venus. Now just as Saturn can be regarded as the dark side of the Moon which leads to the Sun if we have the courage to face our personal shadow, so Jupiter can be regarded as the other side of the Sun which leads to the Moon, which is borne out when we remember that Jupiter is exalted in Cancer, the Sign of the archetypal mother.

Saturn and Jupiter, therefore, represent the general expression of the primal yang-yin energies contained in the Sun and Moon, while Mars and Venus represent the particular expression of those two energies. The evolving child needs to develop his own individuality by asserting his personal power, and needs first to break away from the parental figures in order to realize his Self through the Ego. The ability and the means to achieve this independence and initial separation is through the position of his Mars. He also needs to relate to others as well as to his own 'other half' and his own feelings and emotions through Venus.

The means to achieve these dual ends is through the triad which includes Mercury as the expression of the rational faculties and here, too, the relationship of these three personal energies can be seen on the Tree. Mercury opposes Venus as the rational, conscious side of the mind balancing the intuitive powers. And in its position directly under Mars it can be seen as the mental expression of consciousness in relation to the assertive energy. In theory the child needs both security so that it can express its love and also freedom to express its individuality, and the growth of the Ego is contained in the uneasy attempt to balance these two opposing forces.

Thus Saturn represents the necessary sense of order and discipline that the child needs and Mars the urge to react against this outside structure so that he can develop an individuality of his own and become a conscious human being. If the Saturn principle of structure is either too strong or too weak then the child will be unable to assert himself. As Anthony Storr has written: 'In adult life, the aggressive drive which in childhood enabled the individual to break free of parental domination serves to preserve and define identity.'[15]

If the parents are too harsh or inhibitive, if the sense of duty, discipline and order are too great then the child is unable to express his assertive feelings. Here Mars is overpowered by Saturn. If, on the other hand, there is a lack of effective discipline and structure either because the parents are ineffective or perhaps if one or both is actually missing, then equally the child is unable to express his assertiveness because he has nothing to fight against and no model of strength built into his own character and this situation can be seen in the weak Saturn and the corresponding position of Mars.

If we look at the Sun to begin with we can see the basic image of the father and then his role as the provider of structure and authority can be seen in Saturn. The effect of this authority can finally be seen in Mars. As the Shadow, Saturn represents the disapproval of the parents which is transformed into the personal fears of the individual, and Mars represents his need to fight these fears in order to be independent and live in his Sun. The difficulty in expressing the assertive side of one's nature is as much a general as a personal one, and it is of course perfectly natural to value the qualities of loving and peace more than their opposites.

But the Mars energy is one that needs to be expressed, not only in the original development of the individual in childhood but throughout his life. To quote Anthony Storr again: 'The aggressive drive is an inherited constant, of which we cannot rid ourselves, and which is absolutely necessary for survival.'[16] And elsewhere in the same book he writes: 'Just as a child could not possibly grow up into an independent adult if he were not aggressive, so an adult must needs continue to express at least part of his aggressive potential if he is to maintain his autonomy.'[17] The less able he is to express this energy, the more repressed it becomes and the greater the likelihood that it will be projected negatively onto other people or inwards to the damage of the individual himself.

Once the child has achieved independence through his Mars and has thus gained the confidence to be himself and to live in his Sun as an individual he can learn to relate to others through his Venus. Thus the measure of a person's ability to relate to others and to respect them and love them as people in their own right is closely linked with his own ability to accept himself as an individual in his own right, to be his own authority and to express his own nature. As Eric Fromm has emphasized in his works, it is only when a person genuinely loves himself that he can truly love others.

Venus, then, is a direct result of the individual's Moon as his yin energies derived from the maternal-image through the sense of security and love he obtains from his mother. His desire to please the mother in particular and the sense of warmth and emotional proximity he receives from her is expressed in his own power to love others. Similarly, the way he projects the female image onto others through his anima if he is a man, and the way she feels her own feminine side and expresses her feelings directly through relationships if she is a woman can be seen in the position of Venus as a derivative of the Moon's position.

Although it is valid to see Venus and the Moon, and indeed Jupiter, as separate aspects of the feelings, they should first be regarded as parts of a greater whole. Indeed, if one accepts that the characteristics are derived from the parental images it should be obvious that all the factors in the Birth Chart originate from the same source. This is why it can be dangerous to look separately at the Moon as a symbol of the archetypal Mother-figure and Venus as the archetypal daughter or young woman. In one sense the Moon is the image of the mother and it may well be projected onto the type of women to whom a man is attracted on a long-term basis, while Venus is the image of the type of woman to whom he is attracted on a more immediate, physical level.

But if we accept that the psyche is a whole and that the feminine images in their entirety were all derived from the same source, then we must also see the unity behind the apparent separation. To see the two as independent can lead to the dual attraction of a female in accordance with the Moon image and then, because the Venus image has not been recognized and integrated, the attraction of another woman in accordance with the latter image. Both Venus and the Moon are aspects of the female within each one of us and the two need always to be reconciled by the acceptance of both. Each in their way is a separate energy and represents a separate aspect of the psyche, but for that very reason they must be contained within the individual.

In the same way both Mars and Saturn and the Sun are aspects of the male within each of us and the inevitable contradictions and conflicts within these forces need to be reconciled into the whole for the healing process of the psyche to take effect. As Storr pointed out when he wrote of the Mars force, the energies within the psyche are constants. The immutability of these energies, which remain throughout our lives, can be seen graphically in the Horoscope. How we get in touch with them and transform them is the lesson that each of us has to learn in this game of life.

5 *Transpersonal values and the path to the Self*

Between man and God, there is not only no difference, there is no multiplicity, only one.   MEISTER ECKHART[18]

We now come to the role of the three outer planets – Uranus, Neptune and Pluto. How do these energies, unknown to our ancestors, fit into the model of the psyche? What do they represent in terms of the Self and the spirit? We started in unity and we end in unity. We begin with undifferentiated oneness when we are totally identified with our source, initially with the mother. Here we are unconscious and there is no difference between inner and outer because we have not as yet developed the means to tell the difference. There is at this stage only one world and it is our world – hence we dwell in a universe which is purely subjective.

The aim of therapy is to return to our source, but this time in the full light of consciousness. Instead of the primordial unity where all is one we achieve the union of the whole by accepting all that is within the psyche. By accepting it and containing it, by experiencing each factor in the psyche symbolized by the factors in the Horoscope, by accepting the differences within us that are a result of the original separation of conscious and unconscious, by accepting the conflicts and the tension, we become aware of ourselves.

It is important to appreciate that what we are doing is going round in a circle. We end up precisely where we started – there is nowhere else to go. There is no one else to become. We can only become ourselves. It is *our* Self we seek throughout this life of ours. It is *our* life, and ours alone, that we must live. Thus the Hero on the quest searches for the Grail. But the Grail is within him all the time. He needs only to ask the right question – to accept what is there – for his wound to be healed. This circular path which leads nowhere and everywhere is what Jung called the circumambulation of the Self, and it is this circular path that is symbolized both in the wheel of the Horoscope and in the ceaseless orbits of the heavenly bodies.

This does not mean that we have nothing to do. I have described the goal. How is this goal achieved? The way to achieve the goal is to get in touch with the whole through the parts and that means experiencing all that is within us. Accepting every part of our nature as a valid aspect of our being, both that which we regard as good and that which we think is bad. And experiencing it means consciously working through each part. It is easy to think that because we are whole already we need do nothing, or to believe that as the aim is recognition of what is already contained within us we need only open our eyes.

In a sense this is true. We do need to recognize that which is within us and that is why astrology is ultimately a way of perceiving, a new way of seeing reality and our own selves that are a part of this reality. But it is far from being *only* a question of recognition. Until we experience our nature, our deepest fears, that which we passionately hate, that which we long to love, until we endure the bitter agony of realizing that what angers us and annoys us is a part of ourselves, until we have burned in the fire of our desires and recognized them for what they are, we cannot return to the spirit in the light of consciousness.

We have looked at the separate parts with which we need to be in touch in the previous sections of this chapter. Let us now look at the three outer planets as a means of getting in touch with the whole which is the Self. Everything in the Horoscope leads to the centre and it is absolutely vital that while we are on our journey we bear in mind the ultimate goal. We began with the Sun-Moon polarity as the symbol of the undifferentiated yang-yin principle. The process of development is achieved by developing the Ego, the conscious side of our nature, symbolized by the Sun, so that we can return to our unconscious source, symbolized by the Moon. Then we become consciously in touch with ourselves, with the whole of our being, and then we are whole and the healing process is accomplished.

When we reach this stage the parts of the Horoscope do not disappear. But they are transformed as we have got consciously in touch with them. The role of Uranus then is to break away from the authority of others, to separate the Ego, to begin the process of individuation by cutting off from the restrictions of the past so that consciousness and individuality can be developed. We need separation, space, freedom, objectivity in order to see. To see ourselves and to see others in relation to ourselves. This is the lesson of Uranus, the first step towards the spirit, breaking away from Saturn, soaring up into the sky away from the earth; heaven separating from the ground beneath.

Severing the umbilical cord can be a painful process; leaving the safety of the Garden of Eden with their new-found knowledge and freedom was no easy task for our predecessors. But we can only find ourselves by being ourselves and to do this we have to leave the past behind. For it is only when we have taken this first step of separation that we can see the past, that which we have clung to, in its true light. Sometimes the mind breaks down at this point. Both Freud and Jung suffered breakdowns when Uranus opposed its natal position. Freud saw for the first time his real relationship with his own father – the Saturn figure. Jung discovered himself by breaking away from his surrogate father-figure, from the fixation he had projected onto Freud.

The next stage, once we have developed the Ego consciously by the Uranian process of separation through independence, is to reconcile the Ego through Neptune with the unconscious. This is the search for union, to be at one with our source, with the absolute, or with the spirit. We want once again to be one, to be whole, to blend ourselves with the rest of the universe and humanity as one drop becomes a part of the ocean. We want here to return to Maria – the sea and the mother. Then, having achieved the objectivity to see in our separateness, we can unite the conscious Ego with our unconscious substratum.

And, in doing so, we reach the final stage – that of Pluto, where we are transformed, where we are re-born in full consciousness and where we can recognize our wholeness. Then we return to the Sun, to the source of our inner power and we find our true identity, we become the people we really are. Then the little Sun, the small circle with the point at its centre, becomes the larger Horoscope, the greater circle surrounding the still point. Then the

Ego becomes the Self. That is why Pluto is associated with one's personal identity and with the principle of power – for it is the means to find the power which is contained in potential in the Sun.

So, therefore, in reaching the centre we are centred because we are in in touch with all that is within us, and all that is us. We can see this ideal in the model of the Tree which serves to remind us of the roles of these three outer planets as aspects of the whole psyche. Here we can see the Sun at the centre of the psyche, and here, too, we can see the position of these three bodies. Placed at the top of the Tree they lie beyond normal consciousness and thus they can be regarded as 'transpersonal' values. But they can also be seen as parts of the psyche – lying like all else within the whole.

This, then, is the point. In one sense they do represent something beyond normal consciousness, and yet at the same time, being part of the whole, they should never be thought of as extraneous to the psyche. This indeed is a very real danger. The aim towards psychic wholeness is integration of all the parts into the whole. The Ego becomes the Self. The spirit, the sense of meaning we seek, is within us. It does not lie beyond us. Transformation, which is rightly regarded as the role of Pluto, then leads to transformation of the whole. It leads us back to Paradise – to the Tree in the Garden of Eden which is for the healing of the nations. In the process each factor in our Horoscope becomes transformed and is reconciled into the whole which is the Self.

Once we have achieved this transformation we are back at the beginning. We find the meaning, the spirit if we like, of our lives within ourselves. Saturn is transformed into the Sun but Saturn does not disappear. Instead of being controlled by an outside authority, we become our own authority, we become the authors of our own destiny. Then we embrace our personal cross and find its yoke easy and its burden light. Then it is no longer that which we irrationally fear because we have been unable to face it, but that which supports us.

This is the difference between sublimation and transformation. In sublimation the energy which flows in the troubled area is applied elsewhere in a conscious effort, while in transformation the drive itself is changed and this brings about a change in the unconscious. We can see the difference in the lives of the Buddha and St Francis, on the one hand, and St Paul on the other. Legend has it that the Buddha was made to go through all the pleasures of the flesh so that he would no longer desire them. St Francis, too, lived the life of a profligate until, at the age of his first Saturn return at twenty-nine, he turned to the life of the spirit. He no longer felt the need to possess things and the beauty of his genuine love for humanity, for the earth, the animals and the birds, is in stark contrast to the fanatical zeal of St Paul who, never having accepted his earthly desires, clearly loathed everything to do with the flesh.

When transformation takes place the fear of Saturn no longer troubles us. In sublimation it is repressed and continually affects us in our unconscious. Thus the role of the outer planets is to put us in touch with our real needs, not to try to rise above them or avoid them by seeking the spirit outside. Everyone in his own way needs to find his spirit but at the end of the day this spirit, the meaning of our lives, can only be found by facing ourselves, and as we have seen the first step in that process lies through the symbolism of Saturn – the Shadow. Only when that area of the psyche is fully accepted can transformation and the integrity of the personality be achieved.

I emphasize this point because it is easy to think of these 'transpersonal' values as leading to something beyond one's Self. There is nothing beyond the Self. All that is, all that ever was, and all that ever will be, lies within the Self, within the wheel of our personal Horoscope. This, indeed, is at the root of the divergence in the two basic viewpoints in psychology – the Freudians who are concerned with solving the problems of living, through relationships, work or learning to be more effective in the world and who look with distrust on those who follow Jung and many of the moderns in their search for 'spiritual' meaning, often condemning the latter as unscientific.

But in reality the aims of all therapists, of whatever persuasion they are, are the same. Each in his own way seeks the realization of the Self, the union of conscious and unconscious. The nature of this spirit or meaning will differ for each person is unique and it is *his* meaning that alone is his goal and *his* Self. Some will find this union, or spirit, through relationships and in their work in the world; others will find it through a sense of inner meaning or purpose.

Each person in his own way seeks wholeness, and each in his own way must and can only, find his own wholeness. This does not detract from the 'spiritual' dimension and the name which is given to the ultimate goal does not matter. What does matter is that we recognize where we can find this 'spirit', that we recognize at the last that the temple of God is within us. And that, in this context, the outer planets are a path towards this ultimate goal of wholeness through containment and the acceptance of our Selves in their entirety and not in the search for something beyond.

The outer planets, then, do lead to a new consciousness. But it is not a consciousness of anything new in itself. We are now entering a new Age and the discovery of these forces in the universe is leading towards the realization of the new evolutionary leap that mankind is poised to take. In one sense the universe is the same as it has always been for it is eternal. But eternity embraces change and the universe is a continual process of change. Inasmuch as the universe is our universe and in so far as it changes for us in accordance with our view of it, these energies lead us to see the universe in a new way. As we learn to see in this new dimension which unites change in eternity the universe itself is changed by our perception of it. This, then, is the new consciousness that is embodied in the outer planets, a consciousness that brings about change not only in our own Selves by uniting us, but in the universe itself by uniting us consciously with the universe as a whole.

CHAPTER 5

From Ego to Self – integrating the Horoscope

The beginning exists for the sake of the end.

MEISTER ECKHART[1]

In the last two chapters we looked at the fundamental energies which constitute the psyche in both their ideal and their actual forms. We shall now see how these energies manifest in the Horoscope to produce the unique pattern that is the individual. Traditionally these energies, the Sun, Moon and the planets, are described according to the Signs, Houses and aspects, and the combination of their cycles in the arabian parts, the nodes, mid-points and harmonics.

The way in which the separate factors are placed in the Horoscope describes the divisions that exist in the individual, the conflicts and complexes that together make up his own particular nature. When life is created unity is destroyed and the result is conflict. This conflict is inherent in the division of the original unity and co-exists with it. So it is that we need to be aware of both levels – of the way the factors manifest in the life of the individual through the Signs, Houses and aspects, and also of the way they exist as parts of the whole through the final goal of the psyche in its quest towards the spirit.

If we look at the Horoscope illustrated in Figure 5.1 we see the Sun in Aquarius, close to the I.C. in the 4th House, making a square aspect to Uranus, a sextile to the Moon, a trine to Jupiter. In order to understand these separate parts it is natural to analyse them by looking at them individually. When we look at the Sun's position we can see the image of the father, we can see the

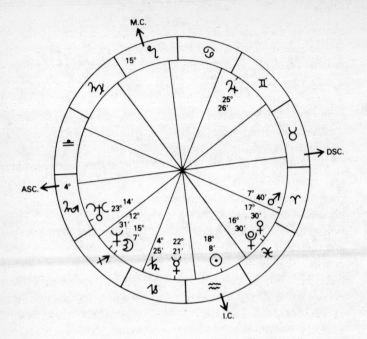

Figure 5.1   *Horoscope of Charles Dickens*

conflicts and potentials that are contained in the Ego, we can see the needs and strivings of the masculine side of this individual.

As we analyse the separate factors we provide a description of a person whose Sun is in Aquarius. As far as it goes this is a useful and convenient way of generalizing. Everyone with their Sun in Aquarius will share a common characteristic just as everyone born in Britain or Bulgaria will share a certain trait. And the person with his Sun in the 4th House and his Sun square Uranus will also share something with others who have those features in their Horoscopes, just as all those who are only children or whose fathers died posthumously will share a common characteristic.

These generalizations are useful, they are convenient, and as far as they go they can be regarded as correct, in a qualified if not an absolute sense. They are useful because we can only see the parts, but the point of looking at these parts is to see the whole through them. Therefore although the Signs, Houses and aspects exist as separate parts of each individual, they are also parts of one unique pattern which is never repeated and which in its totality represents that individual. They are thus ways of perceiving the star under which he or she alone was born.

It is important to stress this point at the outset because what we are trying to discover, when we look at the separate parts, is what they mean to this individual, how they enable this particular person to reach his own Grail. So no one factor in a Horoscope will ever be identical with its equivalent in another Horoscope and therefore there are no fixed, definite meanings to the separate factors. The combination of the various cycles which creates the individual, unique pattern that is the Horoscope is different in every case. My Sun in Aquarius may in a sense be the same as that of Charles Dickens, just as we may both have been born in England, or even Portsmouth. But my Aquarian Sun will never be in the same relationship, through the Houses and aspects, to each of the other factors that exist in the novelist's Horoscope.

We should bear this in mind so that we do not limit our understanding of the individual. Any definition by its very nature limits and this is its aim. The square aspect between Dickens's Sun and his Uranus limits the expression of those bodies by defining their nature and in so doing it enables us to understand the meaning that is contained within those bodies. But the danger of this kind of limitation is that in seeing only the traditional aspects we fail to see that the Sun and Uranus are also factors in the Horoscope as a whole and simply by being parts of the whole pattern they affect each other and each of the other factors, whether or not there are any traditional aspects between them.

1 *Signs and wonders – the Zodiac and the Houses*

> If you have form'd a
> circle to go into,
> Go into it yourself, and
> see how you would do.
>   WILLIAM BLAKE

The planets themselves show the way the psyche is broken down into its constituent parts. The Signs of the Zodiac and the Houses show how these parts manifest in the individual psyche, how the influences are felt by the individual and how he reacts towards them. In this way both the images that affect him throughout his life are laid down and also the consequent conflict that ensues as his emerging consciousness opposes those powerful images that reside within his unconscious.

The Sun, the Moon and the planets all move in their cycles which describe their separate tides and seasons, and we can see the general qualities of the times by looking at the progress of the cycles through the ecliptic and in the way the planets interrelate through their synodic cycles. The Signs describe the cycles of the planets as they appear to move around the ecliptic, the Houses the planetary movement in accordance with the movement of the Earth and the aspects the relationship of the planets to each other which are thrown up in the never ceasing patterns that are created by their motion.

In this section I shall look first at the Signs of the Zodiac and then at the Houses, and in the next I shall look at the aspects. The Signs of the Zodiac are produced by dividing the ecliptic by twelve, in the same way that the year is broken down into twelve months. It has been suggested that because it is possible to divide the ecliptic by other numbers the meaning assigned to the Signs is invalidated. However, this conclusion is borne out neither by logic nor by practice. We can reduce the Signs to 4 by concentrating on the Elements or we can increase their number to 36 with the dekans or 360 with the degrees. What is clear is that not only do the Signs contain meaning according to their own nature, but there is additional meaning provided by these other divisions.

The Signs, then, symbolize the natural expression of the planets through their cycles. They describe the archetypal situations we experience through the various parts of the psyche. When we look at them in terms of original images we see the influences which create the character. When we see them transformed into the character we see how the individual character manifests. Thus the maternal-image in Figure 5.1 is described in essence by the Moon's position in Sagittarius.

Dickens's mother-image at this stage was of someone outgoing, gregarious, friendly, without being emotionally close. The Sign in itself should be regarded as neutral and it does not indicate the personal effect of the image on Charles which is provided both in the House position and to a much greater extent in the aspects the Moon makes to the other factors in the Birth Chart as well as the Moon's position in the Birth Chart as a whole.

In itself the Moon's position in Sagittarius could produce problems in the sense that it is not a natural expression of an archetypal mother and it would suggest some lack of emotional proximity. But the Sign alone does not show whether a particular child will accept or reject such an influence. In theory the Moon's position in Cancer, for example, would be a more natural expression of its potential. However, the fact that some positions are more apposite in one character than another makes it clear that the way the individual regards the influence depends on his innate temperament and varies considerably.

Thus one child may welcome a Sagittarian mother as exciting and exhilarating, while another may react with a feeling of repressed anger against his independent parent. In the same way one child may react with warmth and devotion to a Cancerian mother-image while another may feel oppressed by her over-protectiveness. Dickens himself recognized his mother's kindness, her gallant gaiety and her faithfulness towards his father although as we can see the aspects surrounding the Moon describe a very difficult and ambivalent complex. As a general description of Elizabeth, it is worth noting that others found her companionable, good-natured and pleasure-loving and indeed, a good mother.

While the Signs describe those influences which create the character according to the images that mould the character, both in their primal and their derivative form, the Houses indicate the way in which the individual responds to those influences, or what the individual does about the influences that have moulded his character. Thus they show how we perceive the images and so how we attract other people and events by what we are, or by what we think we are.

Looked at in this way, we can regard the Signs as objective and the Houses as subjective although there is in fact no sharp dividing line between the two. Dickens's maternal-image centred, according to his viewpoint, especially on his personal feelings with the Moon in his 2nd House, while his father's influence, or lack of it, affected the very roots of his being, placed as it was so close to the I.C. in the 4th House.

The subjective, inner nature of the Houses is all the more apparent when we consider what they actually represent in a Horoscope. It may be thought that in discussing the Persona alone in the last chapter and in regarding the sphere of Malkuth or the Earth as one aspect of the psyche in chapter 3, less than due prominence was being accorded to the Houses and the Mundane sphere. I believe, however, that looking at the Houses in these ways brings out their true nature and shows both their real importance and also the vital fact that they are all aspects of one complete cycle, to a far greater degree in fact than the Signs.

The diurnal cycle, which is represented in the Houses, is of the greatest importance both in astrology and in the practical outworkings of the psyche. But while in practice breaking down the ecliptic circle does, in my view, bring about a greater understanding of reality, the same artificial division in the case of the Earth's rotation has detracted from the real meaning of the mundane sphere. It is certainly valid, in one sense, to break down this circle into twelve divisions, but if this division is to be made in terms of the human Horoscope then it is important not to lose the meaning of the cycle as a whole.

In practical terms I believe that we should regard the diurnal circle first and foremost as a totality. This circle in its entirety represents, in Jungian terminology, the Persona, in other words the way in which the individual reacts in a personal manner to those images which have been created through the parental-figures. To a great extent the difference between the diurnal cycle and the planets can be seen in the distinction made among existential therapists between the Self-images and the Self respectively.

The breakdown of this cycle, therefore, shows the different ways whereby the Persona deals with the inner world or images that have been created. We can see the different ways that the world outside is met through the Persona first, in its peculiarly personal response or self-image in the Ascendant, second, in its response to other people through the mirror-image of personal relationships and immediate personal reactions in the Descendant, third, in its identity with the world at large through the individual's ideals and vision in the Mid-heaven, and fourth, in its relationship to its roots and environment in the I.C., and then into what is effectively a further breakdown of these four principles into the separate Houses.

Thus we see that the whole circle is the Persona and what we tend to think specifically as the Persona by equating it with the Ascendant is in reality its focus at the point where the diurnal circle meets the ecliptic. In so far as any circle can be said to have a beginning the emphasis is placed here at the rising point, the point the ancients believed to contain the star under which each individual is born and which epitomised the Horoscope as a whole. Here, too, we can see how we relate in different ways to the different aspects of our environment, including the people and the events that we attract in accordance with this view, and it is this peculiarly subjective viewpoint which is symbolized in this cycle of the Horoscope.

While we can regard the Signs to a great extent as separate in that the fact that my Sun is in Cancer in no way limits the Sign that my Moon or Mars may be in, the Angles and Houses can only follow each other in a predetermined order. So, if my Ascendant is in Leo, then the cusps of all the other Houses must inevitably follow in their consecutive order. Thus the Houses, unlike the Signs, are dependent on one another and inevitably flow into each other.

The traditional approach to astrology produces practical difficulties because in many cases there is no way of knowing in which House a particular factor is contained. First, there is the problem of which system of House division to use, and second, even when a planet is 'in' a House according to one system, it is often regarded as being more relevant to the subsequent one, if it is close to the cusp of the latter. These difficulties are not of course met with in the Signs where a factor will quite clearly be in either one Sign or another.

Part of the reason for these problems arising is because the Houses were artifically divided on the analogy of the Signs into twelve on a theoretical basis and, moreover, on a basis which may have been appropriate for the kind of astrology that was mainly used at the time, i.e. mundane, horary and electional, but which did not reflect the human psyche. In my view, therefore, it is more appropriate to reassess the Houses in the light of the psyche rather than trying to force ancient ideas where they are no longer applicable.

When we regard the Angles and the Houses as part of a continuous circle which represents our reaction to the images formed by the Sun, Moon and planets then we can also see that the planets are not *in* the Houses, but rather that we are looking at the planets *through* the Houses. In other words the Earth's motion is not separate from the motion of the planets themselves, but the two interrelate. So we can see how we define and create our world in accordance with our perception of it. We see what we expect, both from ourselves and others and, as we shall see in chapters 7 and 8, we can see *why* we create the world in this way.

In Figure 4.2, for example, we can see another person with her

Moon in Sagittarius. When we look at the diurnal circle, the Angles and the Houses which are focused through her Ascendant in Libra, we can see how she, as an individual, reacts to this particular kind of mother-image. We can see too, in that context, how her Midheaven is in the archetypal maternal Sign of Cancer and her Uranus is in close proximity to that Angle, as too the other planetary factors fall into place in their positions in the diurnal circle that we call the Houses.

In chapter 2 I mentioned that one of the three accepted prerequisites for a workable system of psychotherapy was to have a rational system that was acceptable to both therapist and patient. And the point was made that, provided this rational system was meaningful, its total accuracy did not matter. The Houses, to my mind, provide such a system so long as we see them as a whole and appreciate their place as one of the planetary cycles among the others. They do not detract from the other cycles for Dickens's Saturn will always be his Saturn and it will always be in Capricorn. That shadow area will have to be met in his life as a whole, even though he will view it from the peculiar vantage point of his 3rd House.

2 *The quincunx of heaven – the aspects and the interrelationships of the planets*

> But the quincunx of heaven runs low, and 'tis time to
> close the five ports of knowledge.
>
> SIR THOMAS BROWNE

Traditionally the aspects describe the relationship that the planets, and the Sun and Moon, the Angles and other bodies, make to one another. If my Sun is at 22 degrees of Cancer and my Moon is at 22 degrees of Taurus there is a distance of 60 degrees along the ecliptic and because 60 is a division of the whole circle of the ecliptic of 360 by the number 6 there is a relationship between these two factors which is governed by the number 6. The theory of Harmonics accepts this basic premise but continues logically to point out that the complete circle of the ecliptic can be divided by any number and thus all the factors will be in a relationship governed by the number that divides their separateness.

However, it is important to appreciate that every factor in the Horoscope is related to every other factor whether or not it is in traditional aspect or aspected by any number according to harmonic theory. These aspects, the traditional and the harmonic, describe a particular kind of relationship between the factors. It is an extremely important kind of relationship but, and this proviso must be stressed, it is not the only kind, and just because it is one kind of relationship we will inevitably be limited by this particular definition if we believe that it alone exists.

First we need to look at the factors in themselves as parts of the whole without regard to any kind of direct relationship. The very fact that my Sun is in Leo and my Moon is in Cancer creates a relationship between these two bodies and it will be necessary to balance and integrate these two primal energies within my psyche simply because they exist in themselves in my Horoscope, quite apart from any specific aspect they make traditionally or harmonically. If, with my Leo Sun, my Moon were in Virgo, the situation would be quite different, once again before we even come to any kind of specific aspect.

Thus every part of the whole is related to every other part of the whole just because it *is* a part of that whole. In the same way every human being is a part of the whole human race and a child's death in Nicaragua affects me whether or not I am related to him by any direct affinity of blood. To press the point a little further because it does, I believe, bring out our tendency toward linear thinking, let us take the analogy of painting. We can either connect two points by line in which case the line itself creates and defines the particular relationship, or we can create a relationship by colour and tone without using lines. If, in a landscape of golden browns and ochres, I introduce a small spot of bright red, that changes the perspective of the whole painting and by itself alters the other colours in the painting.

This is a matter of importance because there is a tendency to think that unless there is some specific aspect between two factors they have no relationship to each other and also that the relationship is only defined by that aspect. The end result is that instead of drawing the parts together into a whole which is the ultimate purpose of psychotherapy, we proceed in the opposite direction and split the whole up to an even greater extent. This will become more apparent when we begin to integrate the Horoscope in chapters 7 and 8.

The natural relationship of the factors, the innate harmony which is contained in them, is symbolized in the Tree of Life which we examined in chapter 3. Here we can see quite clearly that no part stands alone – each is related to the others. By looking at the sephiroth, which correspond to the factors in the Horoscope, we can see where they balance each other, and by looking specifically at the twenty-two paths of the major arcana of the tarot we can see where their natural aspects lie.

This, too, is of the utmost importance when it comes to integration. When we look at the Horoscope we can see the specific conflict that centres round the individual's Saturn, for example. We can see where his particular problems lie. But to discover the general way of integrating the Saturn principle into the psyche as a whole, the need for balancing order and individuality, the need for channelling the assertive energy beneath it and for creating a tangible vessel for the vision and spiritual force above it, can only be seen on the Tree.

By showing how, on the Tree, each apparently separate part of the psyche forms a relationship with every other part, the lack of integration in a personal Horoscope is also brought out. The fact that there is no close aspect of a specific kind linking two factors can be of great importance, as can the lack of a particular form of energy, especially the lack of any factors in a particular Element. Here the problem can quite literally be the inability, or difficulty, in integrating the unaspected factor or the vacant Element and the difficulty is enforced because there is no impetus towards its reconciliation in the Horoscope.

While it is necessary for the individual to experience every part of his being in order to become balanced and whole, nevertheless there will be particular conflicts and complexes within him and it is these specific complexes which are described by the aspects. In order to experience himself as a whole, the individual needs to work through those areas of his personality which are in conflict and by bringing these parts together in the form of a complex the individual is impelled to work on them.

When we look at the aspects, therefore, we see the principles of the psyche that are brought together in the form of a particular complex. We see the conflict that is engendered and what the individual can do with the combination of those energies. The precise way in which they are brought together, or how they are brought together through a specific type of aspect, is of secondary importance.

Let us look briefly at the kind of conflicts that are brought about when the planetary factors are brought into aspect with the personal parts of the psyche. For this purpose I mean by 'personal parts' first, the two primal yang-yin factors: the Sun and the Moon, then, the secondary images of these forces: Mars and Venus respectively, then Mercury, our mental reactions to the world, and finally the diurnal cycle which, for practical purposes, I shall centre on the two convenient points of the Ascendant and the Midheaven.

When Pluto contacts the Sun or Moon the principle of power is brought to bear through the primary male or female sides of the psyche. Thus there is a conflict centred on the question of power which affects the individual's own sense of power or identity. Because what we see in the astrological factors are the images which are introjected by the individual on an unconscious level we cannot see the actual parents, or whoever in practice provided those images, in an objective sense. What we can see is the way the individual perceived his parents.

The two sides of every factor are brought out in their original influences. And by looking through the two sides we arrive at the underlying principle. What the individual feels with Pluto contacting his Sun or Moon is that his personal power, either his assertive power, the ability to be himself, his very identity in the case of the Sun, or his feelings, his emotional response, his feminine side in the case of his Moon, is threatened. The reasons for this influence reflect both sides.

Either he feels overpowered by a dominant parent or he feels the lack of power, a void, in the effective lack of that parent and often Pluto shows either the actual death of a parent and thus a literal lack of his presence or an emotional detachment which cannot be breached. The result in either case is the same. The individual is drawn to that which he feels, rightly or wrongly in an objective sense, that he lacks. And equally he feels the necessity of resisting that which threatens him. So with this position there is an ambivalent feeling centred originally on the parent in his or her role of provider of power.

Thus, if the parent is remote, the child will try to make up for this lack by getting closer. If the parent is the father with a Sun-Pluto contact the child will lack a sense of personal identity and will have a great need to create an identity of his own. This of course was the whole basis of Adler's therapy centred as it was on his own Sun-Pluto square. The conflict, however, is brought out because the individual is attracted by what he lacks in himself through an outside source, and so he will be attracted to an outside source of power which itself will threaten his own identity. Then he will be driven to break away from it. What he really seeks is the source of his own power or identity, but there is always the likelihood that in seeking it through another he will either try to dominate others or he will feel constantly threatened by them.

We can see an example of the Moon-Pluto contact in the Horoscope of Charles Dickens, where there is a close square aspect. This Moon-image is complicated by its other aspects, as the factors are likely to be in an actual case. In itself the Moon-Pluto contact describes a mother who is perceived as either dominating, the archetypal Kali image who threatens to devour her children, or who is remote. In either case the child is driven to try to get close but the proximity which results is also seen as a threat to the integrity of his feelings.

There then develops an obsessional attraction towards women which results in a power struggle. The individual may consciously attempt to retain the identity of his own feelings by effectively repressing them, but in this case there is all the more likelihood of being attracted to a dominating figure and all the more fear of being taken over in a relationship. In so far as the female-image is translated into the feminine image of the individual, whether in the case of a man or a woman, it is transformed into his partners or her feminine side, and onto their feelings in both cases. We can see, for example, the literal transformation of the remote and powerful mother-figure that Henry II had in the Empress Matilda with his Moon in Aquarius square Pluto when he married Eleanor of Aquitaine.

When Pluto contacts the Angles we see the results of the primal parental images as they affect the individual. With Pluto close to the Ascendant the individual reacts to his particular influences by needing to express his identity in a very personal way and to impose his will upon others. He will ask: 'Who am I?' and constantly seek a way to express the personal identity he lacks. Close to the Midheaven his search for identity takes the form of having to succeed or to prove himself in the world by material achievement or making his mark on the world.

If Pluto contacts Venus then the power struggle is brought out in the individual's relationships and the ambivalence of his feelings will be apparent in this area of his life. In Dickens's Horoscope we can see that the primal mother-image is linked directly to his way of relating with Pluto being close to Venus and both being in close square aspect to his Moon. Contacting Mars the conflict centres around his need to assert himself and we can see an example of this in Figure 1.1. Similarly, the contact to Mercury shows that the search for personal power and identity must be resolved through the mind.

When Neptune contacts the Sun or Moon there is a sense of unreality about the respective parent. If we compare this position with contacts by other planets we can see how the subjective nature of these images, as opposed to the objective situation, is brought out. Pluto may mean a real loss as may Neptune. So, too, may Uranus, Saturn or Jupiter. But the way that the child perceives subjectively the same objective fact is what can be seen in the Horoscope. Thus it is what the images mean to him, as parts of his psyche, which is described in these factors. This, of course, is what really matters and it is also made clear that there is no question of blame as far as the actual parents or anyone else is concerned.

If Pluto is in evidence, then there is a powerful void, as if the central core of the personality had been blown out of the psyche. This void needs to be filled by the individual exerting his own power in some way. When Neptune is effective, the lack becomes immaterial. Deprived of a solid basis for the paternal or maternal image, the individual seeks meaning beyond or apart from the material level. And in the lack of the material world, he is forced to create a world of his own imagination, whether it be through religion, art, humanitarian endeavours, esoteric understanding or some form of escapism.

Thus the parent may be weak, elusive, artistic, spiritual or deceptive. As we can see from Figure 5.1 Charles Dickens's mother combined these qualities, at least to that particular child, with the powerful image of the Pluto contact and Neptune being drawn closely into the complex that includes both Moon and Venus.

Dickens felt that his mother had rejected him. As we have seen when we looked at the Signs in the last section, the very fact that the Moon is in Sagittarius indicated a lack of close emotional bonding although this could have meant a genuinely friendly influence. The sense of mystery and falsehood which pervades most of his work, the mixture of play and terror, the imaginative world which was fraught with anxiety, the reality threatened by deception which was central to his imaginative writing had its origins in this aspect of his childhood.

The obsessive fear of being in anyone else's power which affected not only his personal relationships but also his financial and business dealings and which made him distrust others and break away from many of his associates was also closely linked to these parental images. Even his claustrophobic dread of being buried alive and his whole view of the world from the angle of a frightened child which gave him such sensitivity to the plight of others, and at the same time such a fear of chaos inside and out which drove him to support law and order and outer respectability while decrying its practical effects on those who were its victims, can be seen in his internal relationships to the parental figures.

I have deliberately stated that these conflicts were the results of the parents rather than the mother. Dickens blamed his mother because he was sent to work in a blacking facory while he regarded his father with affectionate friendship. It is true that his mother asked for his return to the factory and Dickens was to write later: 'I never afterwards forgot, I never shall forget, that my mother was warm for my being sent back.'

But in many ways his mother did her best with the mess that was left by her husband's impecunious and lazy ways which ensured that he lost what money they had and forced their sensitive child to work in the first place. That the negative feelings were laid against the mother and that they affected his relationships with the women in his life which resulted in an absence of any real sympathy for, or understanding of, the female sex, is as apparent in the position of Venus in this complex as it is in his life and in his work.

We can see the effect of Uranus contacting one of the two primal energies also in Dickens's Horoscope where it forms a square aspect to the Sun. In *Martin Chuzzlewit* the hero says: 'A man is himself and himself alone.' Uranus separates and this, too, can be the literal apartness of a parent, seen in this instance as detachment. Here there is a feeling of tension which in keeping him apart drives him towards the expression of his individuality.

One can also see in Dickens's Birth Chart how the two basic Sun-Moon energies are part of one whole and how the one affects the other. Just because of his ambivalent feelings towards his mother which made him afraid of being overpowered and of being drawn away from reality, he compensated through his Sun-Uranus square by developing his own individuality and his own personality. In fact the way the individual sees one parent is necessarily dependent on the way he sees the other, as we can see from the way Charles himself laid so much of the blame for his attitudes on his mother while retaining a false view of his father who did not have to cope with the problems of day-to-day living as his mother did.

Saturn, which itself is one of the derivatives of the primal male image, lays down in the child the sense of structure and order which is necessary for his sense of security. A contact between this principle and the Sun or Moon shows a feeling of imbalance where this energy is concerned, either because there is too much discipline or where there is a lack of it. Then the individual will be drawn unconsciously towards the principle of authority, but because it is not his authority, and thus deprives him of his own sense of being, he reacts against it. The answer is to find his own authority and his own integrity through the image by experiencing the factor within himself.

Hope and faith are encompassed in the image of Jupiter although the origins of these feelings can be as ambivalent as those contained in any other planetary principle. The child may be filled with optimism because of a very positive influence or he may hope to compensate for the lack of love or security that he needs. Whatever the actual influence, the innate faith in one's abilities will be present and where the other factors in the Horoscope are contacted then that principle will be apparent in their effects.

Similarly, when Mars and Venus contact the Sun and Moon the sense of anger or assertiveness on the one hand or beauty and harmony on the other are centred on these images, just as they are apparent in the particular reactions to the primal images when they contact the other factors in the Horoscope. Naturally when they are also involved with other factors then the complex draws together in a direct form the respective principles – sometimes, as in Dickens's Horoscope, connecting the original influences with the subsequent reactions, thereby providing additional impetus for the individual to work out his conflicts in the course of his life.

3 From the centre – a simplified approach

A student of mine once asked whether a particular factor in the Horoscope referred to the astrology or the psychology. To paraphrase a well-known statement from religion we could say that nothing masks the face of the Horoscope so much as astrology. Although the goal of wholeness is being constantly stressed in astrology, when it comes to the point and astrologers actually look at a Birth Chart all their admonitions fly out of the window. To be fair this is as true of many disciplines. We see the artist who knows that he must capture the essence of his subject and who then starts by drawing the eyes and consequently ends up by getting the whole portrait out of proportion.

Similarly in astrology we are looking at one human being. In the wheel of the Horoscope we are regarding one complete pattern that in its entirety *is* that person. Then what happens in practice? We take the whole to bits, and like some frenetic watchmaker we find we cannot put it back together again. We end up with a mass of meaningless detail that in no way reflects the psyche it once was. And then not content with this plethora of useless minutiae, we create even greater confusion by introducing artificial divisions that exist only in the desperate extremities of our minds.

Astrology is really a very simple system. The basic materials are few and potent. It is natural that when we start we should get fascinated by the variety of techniques that are at our disposal and it is therefore not surprising that we get attached to them. But more complicated techniques do not lead to a greater understanding if they are divorced from their subject matter. Picasso said, in opening an exhibition of children's art, that when he was their age he tried to paint like Raphael. Now he tried to paint like them.

Let us then get down to essentials. What we are trying to do is to understand the human psyche so that the individual can experience it and thereby get in touch with himself so that he becomes integrated and whole. In order to understand this psyche we need to see it. The way to see it is through the Horoscope and thus astrology is, as I have continually stressed, first and foremost a way of seeing. Provided we do see the psyche through the symbolism of the Horoscope it matters not which particular method or technique we use just as in order to heal the psyche it matters not to which particular school of therapy we belong.

Having made this point it must be said that it is easier to begin by looking at the Horoscope in simple terms and then gradually to work through more complicated techniques rather than starting with complicated techniques and then trying to sort through a mass of detail. The reasons why in practice astrologers do not see the unity in the separate factors is first, because they do not look with sufficient depth at the basis factors, and second, because they do not see the connection between them.

Every factor in the psyche reflects the psyche as a whole just as every cell in the human body reflects the complete organism. There are many ways of seeing the same thing. To return to Dickens's Birth Chart, if we want to learn about his parental images we need to look at his Sun and Moon. The basic facts are that his Moon is *there* in his British Chart – in Sagittarius, in the 2nd House; while the Sun is in Aquarius in the 4th House. That is what we need to understand. Those are the facts. What do those factors mean? What do they mean together – as two sides of one force? As the Tao split into the yang and yin energies?

When we go on to describe those factors according to an aspect and in other ways we introduce specific definitions into the relationship that exists between those energies. We can define the relationship by saying that the bodies are close to 60 degrees and that they are therefore in sextile aspect. This aspect is brought out in the 6th Harmonic and we can look at other harmonics to bring out other aspects of the relationship in other ways. We can introduce further combinations – the Ascendant through the part of fortune, the Earth through the Moon's nodes, or we can create an artificial position between the two when we look at their mid-point.

These techniques are all valid in their own way provided they are used in the right way. Once we have understood the actual factors as they are then these refinements can be used to bring out points which are relevant. But all too often the end result lies in the opposite direction of the theory and we end up like the painter whose subject's face is off-balance. The theory of harmonics, for example, is intended quite rightly, as a theoretical concept, to unite the various cycles of the planets in the ecliptic, the diurnal and the synodic. What it does in practice in most cases is to highlight the separate attributes of the aspects which are extracted and separated from the Signs and Houses. So in the end we are in danger of losing sight of the Sun and Moon as they actually are in the Birth Chart and seeing them only through the abstract concept of numbers.

If on the other hand we start with the whole, then we can divide the factors gradually until, if we wish, they can be further refined to bring out a specific feature. Then, however, that feature will remain as part of the whole. So we can start with the Sun and the Moon as the two poles upon which the rest of the psyche exists. Then we can move on to the secondary attributes of these two fundamental forces: Venus and Mars and Saturn and Jupiter and also to the symbol of the mind, Mercury, through which the world 'out there' is processed. And, similarly, we can look at the Angles and the Houses that flow from them as part of one complete cycle. There will then be no need to look at the three outer planets independently save so far as they contact one of the bodies already mentioned.

When we come to the relationships between the planets we will appreciate that we are concerned with the particular conflicts and complexes that are stressed in the individual. In these circumstances we need only be concerned with the so-called 'hard' aspects: the conjunction, square and opposition, and in practice with the close aspects that are made, usually up to five degrees of orb. If we concentrate on the existence of these factors, the importance of what is lacking in the Birth Chart, in the Elements and in the absence of close, hard aspects will also be apparent. Personally I believe that if we wish to understand a human psyche we can use these factors alone to reach that psyche's meaning which leads to its self-realization. If we want to discover further refinements beyond that point, then is the time to turn to other techniques.

CHAPTER 6
All that is – time patterns of the psyche

All that is, at all,
Lasts ever, past recall.
Earth changes, but thy soul and God stand sure.
                                                    ROBERT BROWNING

1 *The development of the psyche in time*
A fool can neither escape the future nor endure the present.
                                                    CICERO

The psyche is not a static entity. It is a process which develops in accordance with its inherent pattern in time as well as in space. We have seen that the aim is to experience ourselves in order to get in touch with ourselves so that ultimately we become whole. This experience can only take place in time, not only because the experience necessarily takes time in a linear sense as therapists from Freud onwards have recognized, but above all because the experience itself is a part of the whole time structure of life.

Each life gradually unfolds according to its own pattern. That unfolding is as much a part of the seed that is born at the time of birth as the pattern of the Birth Chart in space. Psychotherapists have long been aware that their patients undergo certain types of crisis at certain times in their lives and at these times they are more vulnerable to breakdown and distress. Astrology has the ability to provide meaning not only for these general periods but also for the individual periods of vulnerability which are concealed from the therapist.

Therapists have always appreciated that patients need time to experience their conflicts. Freud recognized that at the beginning of treatment he would encounter resistance and only when the initial resistance had been surmounted could the treatment proceed to the next stage of transference, and so through counter-transference until eventually, in the course of time, the contents of the unconscious began to filter through to the conscious mind. The time taken by treatment has indeed been a constant source of practical difficulty in therapy. Given that the patient must experience the contents of his unconscious for himself in order to reach his complexes, the amount of time spent on treament will often be lengthy. In the circumstances ways of shortening treatment have been investigated but all too often it has been found that the understanding which is more immediate has not taken root and once the initial euphoria has worn off no lasting change has been effected.

The reason for this is that experiencing one's complexes involves an innner change, a turning point within the psyche, what may be called a metanoia, or transformation, and it is this that the therapist is in some way trying to bring about through his particular method. By understanding the inherent cycles of time that are within the psyche the therapist can also be aware of the period when the patient is ready for treatment, although this is not usually so much of a problem for the patient will tend to seek treatment when he is ready.

We are part of the natural order and the aim is to evolve into what we are. We have seen the ideal psyche on the Tree. That is the image of eternity where all is perfectly balanced. The way the psyche develops in time is reflected in the Horoscope, for time is the thread that runs through astrology and that enables us to give meaning to our lives. I shall look first at the general pattern of crises, of times of change, in the human psyche. These reflect those that occur in nature as a whole.

Then I shall look at the specific crises that individuals pass through which are reflected in the Birth Chart. Just as there are tides and seasons which exist in the universe and which can be seen in the interrelating cycles of the heavenly bodies, so there are tides and seasons which exist within each separate psyche and which reveal the pattern of that individual as it unfolds from birth to death. And just as each life has its own quality and meaning, so each moment has its quality and meaning. The art of understanding the nature of time is to ensure that the former is brought out in the latter.

2 *The now of time – crises of development*

But take away the now of time, and you are everywhere and have the whole of time.

MEISTER ECKHART

Psychotherapists are aware that at certain times in the lives of everyone there are potentially traumatic transitional periods. These periods they have termed 'crises of development'. Such are adolescence, menopause, the onset of old age, and they are part of our normal and inevitable development. The therapist may also note other specific cycles in time that recur in patients' lives. Freud, for example, who was particularly interested in the power of numbers, was impressed by the fact that he reached creative peaks at seven year intervals.

The menopause, or 'mid-life crisis' as it is sometimes called, has been the subject of particular note. Dr Jacobi has written: 'The basic facts of the psyche undergo a very marked alteration in the course of life, so much so that we could almost speak of a psychology of life's morning and a psychology of its afternoon.'[2] And Jung found this apparent turning point in the middle of the life of especial significance.

It is the therapist's task to try to alleviate the distress of his patients which is likely to be most apparent both at these times of general crisis and at the times of individual crisis which we shall examine in the next section. But without being aware of the meaning of these times, it is difficult to do more than treat the symptoms. What the astrologer is peculiarly able to do is to discover the meaning of these periods both in general and also in terms of the individual who is suffering them.

The times of general crisis correspond to the cycles of the planets in their own revolutions and thus they reflect the continuous cycle of change that exists in the universe and in life as a whole. The seven year cycle which is well known to psychologists reflects Saturn's motion from conjunction, to square aspect, to opposition, to its second square and back to its original position when its cycle repeats itself over and over again. Thus, depending on the speed that Saturn passes through its cycle, everyone encounters a major crisis at about the age of twenty-nine and fifty-nine and minor crises at the seven-year periods between these times.

Jung stated that the aim of the psyche is transformation rather than sublimation. This is the clue to the apparent paradox which is contained in the fact that on the one hand the Birth Chart remains the same throughout life, while on the other we need to be aligned to the constantly changing planetary cycles which affect us from day to day and from year to year. The purpose of all these crisis times is to enable us to experience the inner meaning of the planetary energies as they are in our Horoscopes which reflect our nature in its potential. We cannot change them in the sense of turning them into something else. But we can change their direction.

The lessons that need to be learned relate to all the planetary energies and all need to be assimilated. The complexes that centre on any particular energy naturally vary from individual to individual and it is these that can be seen in the Birth Chart. We all have conflicts, problems, complexes which we need to face and acknowledge. The directions[3] that occur show when we meet them and thus when we can transform them.

It is also necessary to assimilate the planetary meanings in turn. When we look at the energy and the cycles of the planets we can see the point of the relative times they take to pass around the Horoscope. Without the self-confidence of Jupiter we are unable to realize our inner authority which stems from Saturn and it is only when we have attained the authority from Saturn that we can gain the real freedom that comes from Uranus. This is why so few people are able to assimilate the two outer planets, Neptune and Pluto, for they have never succeeded in integrating the others.

Jupiter enables us to have faith in ourselves, to accept God's gifts and thereby to accept ourselves as we are so that we have the confidence to become the people we are. Saturn enables us to find our own authority by facing the shadow area of our lives, that which we fear the most. And these two principles illustrate most effectively the alternating tides of the times – those periods when the energies flow outwards, and those when they ebb. There will always be times when we need to go out with assurance and expand in one direction of life. And there will be times when we need to look inwards and face ourselves.

The principle and paradox of time is most clearly brought out in the contacts of Saturn, the god who ruled time. The obvious paradox is often missed with the result that we fail to experience the true meaning of the crisis. It is frequently said that at the time of the Saturn Return, at the ages of twenty-nine and fifty-nine, we are most free to be ourselves. However, the principle of Saturn is restriction which is the opposite of freedom. How then can we be most free when we are most inhibited?

What happens at these times is that we are driven into ourselves and we are indeed restricted. There is usually a feeling of intense frustration, of being bound down. And it is the very sense of frustration, of not being free, that leads us to react and so to try to shake off the outside authority that is symbolized in the original Saturn influence and that in his own way the individual feels so keenly. What happens at that point is what differentiates true experience from the negative reaction to Saturn's influence.

Some people will simply relinquish existing circumstances – spouses, jobs, homes, and break away from their present lives. But if this is just a negative reaction to the feeling of frustration through an outside authority which they have failed to resolve, the end result will be that they merely get attached to the same circumstances in another guise. So they marry again on the rebound, usually someone who is the mirror image of the spouse they have left. Or they take another job and find they are no less restricted than before.

If, on the other hand, they experience the restriction for what it is, and in so doing come to recognize the true meaning of the authority principle, then in the midst of their suffering, they will be able to emerge from it and transform the principle. Then, instead of reacting negatively to an outside authority, they can become their own authority. The point is that the Saturn principle cannot be avoided. Like any other principle in the individual's nature it needs to be faced and experienced by working through it. And because Saturn represents the Shadow the experience of facing this area will be especially traumatic. But having faced the area through this crisis the individual will be able to experience the freedom of finding himself.

While all the planetary contacts provide us with the opportunity to make a meaningful inner change in our lives, the planet which is specifically associated with change is Uranus. The time of the most potent change is the so-called 'mid-life crisis' at about the age of forty when Uranus opposes its natal position. The Uranus Return, too, at about the age of eighty-four is a time of very real change, but as this is usually the time of that great change from our earthly existence to another, the time 'when we shall all be changed' at the moment of death, it is hardly a time of learning in the mundane sense for the majority of people.

It is the 'mid-life crisis' that Jung referred to and that Dr Jacobi mentions in the quotation above. It is commonly said that this is a change of direction from the first half of life, from the outgoing, yang period to the inner life – the yin period, and that it is the failure to make this necessary change that leads to common distress. So it is at this point that we are forced to face our 'other half' through the anima or animus.

While this may be true in theory and is true in many cases in practice, the real need is to experience the 'other half' of oneself, whether or not it is the extrovert or the introvert side. It is in practice not only those who have failed to get in touch with their feelings in the first half of life who undergo this crisis, but also those who have not fulfilled their active nature.

What the individual feels at the time of the Uranus opposition is a great sense of tension that makes him want to break away from his past. But this may either be a past which has not provided the freedom he sought or a past he no longer believes to be appropriate. So in practice the actual situation at this time is often similar to the crisis the individual undergoes at the time of his Saturn Return. And as all the planetary contacts in their own way are trying to enforce the same ultimate goal, to enable the individual to be more in touch with himself as a whole, this is hardly surprising.

So here, too, we are driven to face the mirror image that may have been avoided in the past and that now makes itself painfully apparent. It was at this time that Freud suffered a nervous breakdown and was driven to face his real feelings about his father. And Jung, too, broke down – and also found himself by freeing himself from the father-fixation he had attached to Freud. The need is indeed to be free. But freedom does not consist of running away from oneself. On the contrary, the metanoia which needs to be achieved at this time is to enable us to reflect that other half which has hitherto remained hidden. Then we can undergo a true change of outlook and be transformed.

Then, finding ourselves, finding the true freedom which is our individuality, we can proceed to the Neptune stage and put our faith in God. Then we can face the void without fear or holding back. Then we can jump into the waters with perfect trust knowing that, having found ourselves, we have nothing to lose. Having nothing we have everything and having everything we want nothing. Then, at the last, we can meet our deepest, most hidden parts in Pluto. Then, having committed ourselves into the hands of God, the veil of the temple which is our inner selves can be torn in two and we can be reborn.

3 *Call back yesterday – crises of accidents*

O! call back yesterday, bid time return.

SHAKESPEARE, *Richard II*

While everyone experiences the crises of development at approximately the same time in their lives, everyone also experiences other crises which can occur at any time in the life-span. These are the results of some specific incident – loss of job, bereavement, physical illness, marital breakdown. It is these latter experiences, which apparently happen out of the blue for no discoverable reasons, that therapists have called 'crises of accidents'.

For the materialist therapist, who sees no connection in what occurs 'out there' in the world and what takes place within the human psyche these are indeed accidents. A woman's marriage breaks down, she suffers psychological stress as a result. She may also suffer physical illness and both, the physical and psychological aspects of her crisis, are treated in the same way. She is given support so that she can get over the problem. The symptoms are treated and patched up and she lives to fight another 'accidental crisis'.

Those therapists who look deeper recognize that there is significance in these apparently random occurrences which reflects the connection between the psyche and what happens in the world, and that the complexes which are brought out at these times can fulfil a useful function. But while it is possible to see a general pattern reflected in everyone in the 'crises of development' there is no way for the therapist to see how the individual psyche is developing and will develop in time. In reality these so-called accidents are just as much a part of the innate development of the psyche as those we have just examined.

If we accept the thesis that the psyche's goal is to realize its self and that in order to do so the individual must experience and reconcile every part of himself, that in the process he must evoke from the unconscious those elements which have been repressed and devalued, his deepest fears and hatreds, the negative associations that exist through what can only be a very painful process, then we can see that these 'accidental crises' are also examples of the necessary and inevitable attempts by the self-regulating psyche to reach its inherent goal.

What we need to do, therefore, is to find what these crises mean to the individual, how they relate to his life, bearing in mind that life exists in time. How then do we reconcile the events which we appear to meet on our life's journey with that life itself? How do we relate the experiences the individual has to the individual who has these experiences? It is all too easy to fall into the trap of looking at the planetary contacts as isolated events. Then when we look into the future we still see only a series of isolated occurrences rather than a meaningful process. What actually happens when the planets contact the Birth Chart is that the individual is being driven to realize the potential that is contained in his Birth Chart. He needs to experience what is there and it is at the times when the planets contact his Horoscope that he will be brought face to face with himself.

There are two main kinds of planetary contact that are used by astrologers. The first progresses the planets in the Birth Chart in a symbolic way, for example on the basis that one day is equivalent to one year. So the planetary positions in the thirtieth year after birth can be seen by looking at the positions of the planets thirty days after birth. As it is only the faster planets that can move far on this basis, the emphasis here is on the Sun, Mercury, Venus and Mars.

The second method is to look at the planets as they are placed in the sky at the actual time under consideration and then seeing what contacts are made by those planets to the Birth Chart. With this system the emphasis is more on the outer planets, as the inner planets move so quickly that their effect is ephemeral. In this way we can see how the individual is brought into contact with the various kinds of reality emphasized by the Humanist-Existential therapists, whereby he meets his inner world in the progressions and his environment and other people in the transits.

When we look at the total situation we realize that the two kinds of planetary contact amount to the same thing, for in reality the world 'out there' and the world 'in here' are two aspects of one entity. We progress each according to our own individual pattern. The inner pattern can be seen by using what we commonly call 'progressions'. But the transits, which apparently reflect the outside world are also a part of our innate development. We ourselves are a part of our environment. We ourselves are a transit – indeed the Birth Chart is literally the transit of our parents. And we can see simply by looking at a Birth Chart how the individual will develop according to both systems and therefore how he will be brought to meet the various aspects of his environment – inner as well as outer.   ·

So if we look again at Rosalind's Birth Chart in Figure 1.1 we can see that at about the age of twenty-one Saturn crossed over her Sun and when she was fourteen Saturn passed over her Moon. Those contacts were as much an intrinsic part of her inner development as the contacts made by the progressed planets. The way in which the contacts operate may appear to affect her more on an inner level in the case of progressions and on an outer level in the case of the transits but the experience that she needs at these times will be the same.

Those experiences will inevitably centre on her Birth Chart for that is the reflection of her psyche. Rosalind has her Sun, Moon and Saturn in hard aspect[4] with the three bodies forming a T-Square. That is an important complex in her nature. It is one cross she has to bear. Whenever a planet contacts one of these three factors making up that complex it will contact the whole pattern. Indeed, if we regard the Horoscope as a whole, then whenever a planet contacts any part of the Birth Chart it will contact the others, in that they are also parts of the whole.

Another important complex in Rosalind's Birth Chart is her Mars in the 12th House square Pluto. To a great extent these two complexes reflect each other and symbolize the difficulty she has in expressing her assertiveness which has been blocked. This is apparent when we bear in mind that both the primal yang force, the Sun, is involved as well as Mars, the secondary force of that principle.

We can therefore simplify the situation when these crises occur. The aim is for the individual to realize the contents of his Birth Chart. At times of crisis the conflicts that exist there are brought out so that they can be faced. The individual then has three choices. He can either avoid them, or he can use them negatively or he can use them positively. If he avoids them then the crises will be repeated throughout his life. If he reacts negatively by using the energy but in an inappropriate way then the result is likely to be more invidious. To illustrate the difference let us compare Hitler with Charles Chaplin who shared certain similarities in their Birth Charts as they were born within a few days of each other. Both had Saturn close to their Midheaven making a square aspect to Mars and Venus in Aries although Chaplin also had the Moon brought into the pattern as part of a T-Square. Hitler never managed to integrate either his Saturn or his Venus-Mars contact in a positive way and although he sublimated these energies and became an authority in a very real sense his fall was all the more devastating in the end. Chaplin, on the other hand, by working through a series of very negative relationships did finally manage to express his feelings positively.

It is especially at these times of accidental crisis, when the client is at his most vulnerable, that he is in a position to learn. This is even more true where a distinct pattern can be seen to be emerging. When relationships continually break up, where the same kind of event appears to recur for no reason. It is then, especially, that the astrologer as therapist can guide the client to realize his true self as well as giving the necessary support to bring him through the traumatic period. For it is then that these accidental crises can be seen in their real perspective as part of the personal cycle of the individual. Then the client can begin to learn what the crises mean to him in the context of his life as a whole.

4 *Growth and change – coincidence in the individual life*

> This grain has in its nature to become rye, that one's
> nature to become wheat, and it never rests until is has
> attained that nature.

MEISTER ECKHART[5]

Rosalind's self is symbolized in her Birth Chart. The way she becomes that self is through the crises that she will meet throughout her life. Every crisis, symbolized by each planetary direction, is part of the process whereby she is enabled to experience her self. The paradox we face in life is that we are ourselves and yet we have to go through a continual process of change in order to become ourselves.

Rosalind was born with the Birth Chart we saw in Figure 1.1. She will die with precisely the same Birth Chart. Why then does she have to change continually when she remains the same during the entire span of her life? The answer is that we can only become ourselves by experiencing ourselves, and this experience only comes about through the crises of change. Thus the crises do not change our nature which always remains the same. But they do enable us to realize that nature in the literal sense of making it real to us. So it is that at these times of crises, reflected in the planetary directions, we are given the opportunity to experience, and to make real, the various elements of our nature.

If we appreciate the purpose of the crises which we inevitably meet in our lives then we can learn from them and, moreover, we can learn to see them as part of the pattern which links the psyche of the individual to the world outside. This unity of perception is one that was inherent among our ancestors and that was at the very basis of astrology. It is largely because we have lost it that we see the crises as extraneous circumstances and so fail to assimilate them in our lives.

Rosalind needs to experience her Birth Chart in its wholeness. Every planetary direction is in its own way impelling her towards the same end. While the 'crises of development' occur at about the same time in the lives of everyone, the meaning for the particular individual will not be the same. And while the principles of the planets is similar at their archetypal level for each person, the way they need to manifest in the life of any particular individual will also be peculiar to that individual depending on his Birth Chart as a whole.

When we combine the 'crises of development' with the 'crises of accidents' we can see how the general and the particular coincide in the individual life. In Rosalind's Birth Chart, as we have seen, the Sun, Moon and Saturn form a T-Square. Whenever Saturn contacts her natal Saturn, and especially at the ages of twenty-nine and fifty-nine when the important Saturn Returns occur in the lives of everyone, it will also automatically contact her Sun and Moon and it will therefore affect her on a personal level. Indeed, every time any of these factors is contacted the complex which is contained in that pattern will be triggered off.

Moreover, the 'crises of development', although they occur at the same time in everyone's lives and thereby reflect the same general pattern, do not take place in isolation. When we look at people's lives we see that at the time of the first Saturn Return, for example, some achieve public prominence while others get divorced; some give up their careers, others die. This is not just a matter of using the crises in the right way. It also reflects the individual pattern in time that is different in each person.

In order to see this individual pattern, and thereby give meaning to the crises, it is necessary to look at the planetary contacts as a whole, as well as relating them specifically to that individual's being as reflected in his Birth Chart. When Uranus opposes its natal position at the time of the 'mid-life crisis', for example, its meaning to the individual will depend first, on the simultaneous contacts that are made by the other planets to the Birth Chart, and second, on the nature of the individual psyche itself as symbolized by the Birth Chart. In one case the Uranus opposition may be preceded by Jupiter's transit of the Moon and followed by Pluto opposing Venus. In another Uranus may contact Saturn concurrently if Saturn is square Uranus in the Birth Chart, and it may then be followed by Neptune crossing the Midheaven.

When we are in touch with time, as we should learn to be by looking at the planetary contacts creatively, we are aware that the pattern of time is a living process which flows according to its own rhythm and cycles. Life in all its forms evolves gradually in time. Season follows season in a natural progression, autumn fading into winter, spring blending into summer. Spring does not suddenly erupt at the vernal equinox nor does the menopause suddenly happen on the day Uranus opposes its natal position.

Although events do happen and these events may synchronise exactly with a planetary contact, if we see only the event we miss the point of what is occurring. One day I took my daughter swimming. As I drove out of the car park at the exact moment that the Moon in Sagittarius was conjunct Uranus, my daughter sneezed violently, I backed the car into the one behind and a girl shot past on a frenzied horse. A person may have a breakdown at the exact moment that Uranus opposes its natal place, but we shall not help her to understand the meaning of that occurrence in her life as a whole if we look only at its moment of manifestation in isolation.

It is easy to assume that if Uranus makes a contact with the Birth Chart it will only have relevance when Uranus is part of a complex in that Birth Chart or if it contacts the individual's natal Uranus. However, it is essential to realize the principle of the planets *in the context of the Birth Chart*. If we do not appreciate this then there will be a real danger not so much of avoiding the principle of Uranus but of using it in the wrong way, in other words in a way which is inappropriate for that individual.

The way that is appropriate for the individual is the way that is described by the individual's Birth Chart. That, and that alone, is how the individual needs to experience the crises that occur throughout his life. In Rosalind's Birth Chart Uranus does not form part of any complex and thus it is not an ostensible problem area. Nevertheless, when she is thirty-eight she will undergo the same 'mid-life crisis' that we are all subject to.[6]

Like every other crisis it will enable her to experience the various aspects of her nature which remain unrealized, not the Uranus principle as an isolated entity, but as part of her whole psyche. In Rosalind's case the major conflicts centre on the inhibition of her assertive needs and the expression of her feelings with the Sun-Moon-Saturn T-Square and the 12th House Mars square Pluto. As the individuality and spontaneity of Uranus have been repressed, this crisis may fill her with a desire to break away from the fixed patterns of her past.

But unless she realizes what is happening in the context of her self as a whole she is likely to miss the real point of the crisis. She may well feel the tension that demands more space in her life but the point is not just to break away from existing conditions. She cannot break away from herself. The point is to bring about the inner sense of change which enables her to accept her own authority that is embodied in the Saturn and Pluto complexes. Then she will be able to express herself in *her* own way. Thus, paradoxically, in her case the Uranus principle of freedom means accepting her own authority by expressing the Sun and Moon through her Saturn. This is her freedom, and it is that freedom alone which she needs to find by getting in touch with *her* self.

All too often, and all too sadly, people are only brought closer to their real needs through the traumas of suffering which occur at the times of the developmental or accidental crises. In the sense that the suffering which is entailed in actually going through these crises is an inevitable part of working through and experiencing ourselves the suffering does not matter. In so far as the suffering brings nothing but bitterness from its distress then its purpose is wasted and so much that might have been fulfilled in a person's life is also wasted.

The nearer we are in touch with the cycles that weave the patterns of our lives the nearer will we be able to move with the universe in perfect harmony with ourselves and with those around us. Then we become centred and then, being centred, we are automatically in touch with time. When we look around us we see people who have an innate knack of doing things at the right time. With them everything falls into place. They are instinctively at the right place at the right time and they move with the effortless grace of a dancer.

And we see others who always, inevitably, do everything wrong, and whose world falls about them dragging misery and pain in its wake. Life and time is a two-way process. The more we are in touch with our Birth Charts, the more we are in touch with time. And the more we are in touch with the world around us, the more in touch we are with ourselves. Then we discover the true art of the seer, he who sees the future to enable the individual to live his future. Then that future becomes the eternal present, the goal that is also the way.

CHAPTER 7
Astrotherapy – the theory

1 *The secret story*

> In many cases of psychiatry, the patient who comes to us
> has a story that is not told, and which as a rule no one
> knows. To my mind, therapy only really begins after the
> investigation of that wholly personal story. It is the
> patient's secret, the rock against which he is shattered. If I
> know his secret story, I have a key to the treatment. The
> doctor's task is to find out how to gain that knowledge.
>
> C.G. JUNG[1]

The secret story that Jung talks of is symbolized by the client's
Birth Chart. First we need to find out how to gain the knowledge
which leads to the understanding of the client's secret story. That
story is the theme of the Birth Chart. The first step, which I shall
deal with in this chapter, is finding that theme through the Birth
Chart. The second, which will be the subject of the next chapter,
is to enable the client to experience his story for himself.

Such, then, is therapy: to understand the story and to enable the
client to experience that story for himself so that he can become
himself. In this sense the first step is for the benefit of the therapist,
while the second is for the benefit of the client, although in reality
the one leads intrinsically to the other. This, too, Jung made clear
when he continued: 'Clinical diagnoses are important, since they
give the doctor a certain orientation; but they do not help the
patient. The crucial thing is the story. For it alone shows the
human background and the human suffering, and only at that
point can the doctor's therapy begin to operate.[2]

How do we find this secret story, the client's theme? So far in this book we have looked at the parts, the separate factors in the Horoscope which together make up the whole. Now we must learn to see the whole. And in doing so we must again stress that seeing the whole is not just a question of putting the parts together again, but of learning to see in a new way – learning to see as a whole. Thus the emphasis is not so much on what we see but on the way in which we see it.

We need to learn to see in a new way. The traditional way of analysis, of breaking down the whole into its constituent parts, is valid as far as it goes. This approach was innate in Freud's method, in the term 'psychoanalysis', and to be fair even in Jung's 'analytical psychology', perhaps an unfortunate term for this very reason. This way leads to diagnosis, and as Jung quite rightly states, diagnosis is important. But we need to get beyond diagnosis. We need to see the client's essence, his Self as Jung would have it, and we need to enable the client to get in touch with, and thus to become, that Self.

By concentrating on analysis, astrology has remained at the level of diagnosis. It is for this reason above all that astrology has not so far been used as therapy. It is for this reason that the potential of astrology has so far remained unrealized. And in failing to realize this potential astrology has failed to reflect the new perception of the universe which it brought into being and which is now once again being realized as we emerge into the dawn of a new Age and a new consciousness.

The parts which I have described in earlier chapters do of course exist in their own right. But these parts are all parts of the whole just as the planets are all parts of one solar system and the various aspects of the psyche are all attributes of one psyche. It is for that reason that I began with the planets on the Tree of Life. Here we can see clearly that the apparently separate principles of assertiveness, expansion, love and fear are all attributes of the psyche as a whole. We cannot therefore look at the principle of love, or Venus, in isolation nor can we solve the problems and conflicts that centre on a person's relationships in isolation.

If we look at Figure 7.1 we see the Birth Chart of Alicia. The various components of her psyche are symbolized in that Birth Chart. We look at her Sun in Aries in the 10th House conjunct Mars and Venus and opposite Neptune. We see her Moon in Aries also opposite Neptune. We see her Cancerian Ascendant and her Mercury in Pisces making a close square aspect to Uranus. These are all separate parts of Alicia's psyche. As such they are conflicting and confused. She herself was confused. She asked for help because she said that although she was very successful in her career, her original words being: 'I am very happy in my work', as the editor of two magazines, she had suffered constant trouble with her relationships.

Seeing the parts does not invalidate the real meaning of those parts. Seeing the parts helps us to diagnose the problems. But seeing the parts only as parts, and giving fixed meanings to those parts does not enable the client to get in touch with herself. The point is to see the whole in these apparently separate factors, to see how they, in their unity, reflect the theme of the individual. To see both through the parts and the innate connection between the parts. So when we look at a Birth Chart, and so the human being who is represented in that Birth Chart, we need to see his story in his conflicts, to see the unity in the broken pieces, to see the individual's theme or spirit in the manifestation of his characteristics. In this way we learn to heal him by making him whole.

Modern archaeologists, having lost the vision possessed by our ancestors, have argued as to whether the Egyptian religion was monotheistic or polytheistic. On the one hand it appears that the Sun alone was worshipped as the one God. On the other a multiplicity of deities abound forming a vast pantheon of celestial beings. The Sun was Khepera at its rising, Ra at mid-day, Atmu when it set. But in reality all the gods were attributes of the one God. Shu, the Sun, was the right eye of Temu, while Tefnut, the Moon, was the left. In the story of creation Temu, having

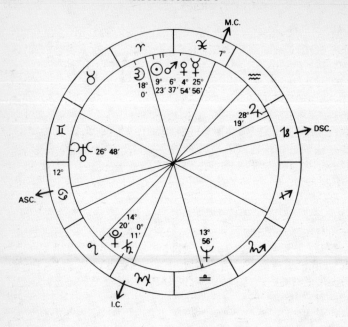

Figure 7.1   *Horoscope of Alicia*

described how Shu and Tefnut proceeded from himself, relates: 'Thus from one god I became three.' It is admittedly difficult for us, so used to seeing in broken images, to perceive as a whole. But modern science itself now recognizes that the separate sub-atomic particles exist only as parts of each other as each reaches out to its fellow.

If we are to achieve the goal of therapy and help the client to become whole then we must learn to see him as a whole. We must learn to see the interconnectedness of the separate parts, the relationship between them, how they co-exist. Then we can see behind the conflicts that manifest on the surface and we can see what they mean to the individual client. Then we can see that, while Alicia's Sun in Aries shares a general meaning with any Sun in Aries, nevertheless it is also a unique part of the pattern which is her Birth Chart as a whole and that its meaning will depend on the other factors which make up her unique pattern.

We can then ask: 'What is the meaning of this factor to this individual?' 'What does it mean to her in the context of the other factors?' 'What is its relationship with the other factors which in their entirety make up this individual?' Then, too, we can see that one area of a person's life is not divorced from the other areas and we can begin to look behind the client's statement that she is fulfilled in her career on the one hand but frustrated in her attempts to relate on the other.

Even if we are concerned with only one specific area of a person's life, with her career or her relationships, it is still essential to begin by looking at the client as a whole. Career and relationships are not isolated aspects of a person's being. Each is an attribute of that person as a whole. Alicia began, as we have seen, by saying: 'I am very happy in my work.' She had a degree in English and, after working in various publishing houses, she became the editor of two magazines. Then she went on to say that she was seeking help because of her 'emotional difficulties' and she described a series of 'disastrous' relationships.

Now it may be that in her particular case her only, or main, problem focuses on relationships. She may well be quite happy and totally fulfilled in her career. She, like all other clients, is unique and she should be treated as such. On the other hand when a client comes for help, he or she may be unaware of the real problem. He may be unaware that there is a problem. And he is certainly likely to be unaware of what lies behind his problem, where his real conflicts lie. In whatever ostensible form the problem takes, at the end of the day, as Anthony Storr remarked, everyone is asking the same question. Everyone seeks to know who *they* really are, and where their secret story lies.

This, after all, is the whole point of astrology when properly used. To see behind the outer, often mundane, circumstances with which the astrologer is presented, to find the real trouble. A man loses his job, has an accident, his marriage breaks down. He may think that there is just something wrong with his job, his health or his marriage. He may or may not be right. What we need to do is to ask: 'Why?' Why did he lose his job? Why did he have this accident? Why has his marriage broken down? What needs does he have? Are those needs being fulfilled? And if they are not, then why not? What conflicts have led to these problems? How do they lead us to discover his story?

The tendency in traditional astrology is to separate, to dissect the psyche through the Birth Chart into neat and tidy categories, usually with the euphemistic excuse that in doing so one is being 'scientific'. So when we want to examine a person's career we look at the Midheaven, at the 10th House, we even take the ruler of these factors into account, perhaps we also look at Mars to see the person's method of work. Then when we are interested in relationships we look at the 7th House, at Venus, perhaps at Mars again for the physical sex drive and so on.

This approach destroys the essential unity of the individual; it destroys his or her essential humantiy and desecrates the spirit of that human being. Moreover the end result, like any attempt to categorize individuals, leads in the opposite direction. It may be convenient to label people, whether they be Cancerians, Librans or Ariens, whether they be Negroes, Jews, Russians or CND supporters, but it does not help to understand them as people.

First we need to approach the Birth Chart as a whole. To see the conflicts, the problems and the potentials that exist within the individual. Then we need to see how the potentials can best be expressed, how the conflicts can be transformed in the individual's life. Every factor in the Birth Chart will, as a part of the whole person, affect every area of that character's life. Everyone needs to face the Shadow in their Saturn. Why is Alicia afraid of physical intimacy with her Saturn in Virgo? This factor, taken in the context of the other factors of which it is an integral part, may have as much bearing on her relationships and indeed on her career and the other areas of her life as the 7th or the 10th Houses.

It may or may not be necessary to bring this out directly in a particular case. But in order to understand the psyche as a whole, it is essential that we perceive it as a whole.

2 *The fight begins – how the parts are connected*

No when the fight begins within himself,
A man's worth something.

ROBERT BROWNING *Bishop Blougram's Apology*

At the end of the last section I asked *why* Alicia had her Saturn in Virgo. If we are going to understand a person's problems and their conflicts we need to know why they exist in that particular form. Similarly, if we are to understand a Horoscope, which reflects that person, we need to know why the various factors in his Horoscope exist in that form.

The tendency to see the factors in the Birth Chart only in terms of function has ensured that astrologers have not understood the meaning of the person's complexes and in failing to do so they have not been in a position to heal them. The approach I am going to adopt in this first stage of understanding the psyche is to look at every factor in the Birth Chart and ask 'why?'. Why does that factor exist in the Birth Chart in the context of the others?

If we just look at the factors in terms of function and character we are no nearer the individual's secret story. The reason is that we enforce the separation between the different components of his psyche instead of uniting them. We look at Alicia's Sun in Aries and say that she is assertive and impetuous. Then we look at her Sun in the 10th House and say that she is ambitious and career-orientated. Then we look at the Neptune opposition and say that she is idealistic and liable to self-deception. We see her Cancerian Ascendant and note her maternal instincts and her tendency to be emotionally self-defensive in her approach to others.

Now, it is quite true that Alicia is a mixture of all these traits and the others that are reflected in the separate factors in her Birth Chart. Up to a point it may be of some use to make the client aware of the differences within her. Usually the client is perfectly well aware, indeed painfully aware, of the differences. What she wants to know is what she can do about them, and above all, what they really mean to her. Alicia knows only too well that her relationships have been a disaster and that she has been successful in her career.

The way to bring about this awareness is not to look at the Sun's position and describe that and then to look separately at the Ascendant and describe that as if they were two isolated parts of this individual. This indeed is what the use of 'sub-personalities' that some therapists advocate encourages, and the tendency has unfortunately been picked up by some astrologers who have thereby encouraged a schizophrenic view of reality.

To discover the meaning of the factors in their essential wholeness we should first look at Alicia's Sun. Then we should look at her Ascendant and ask 'Why has she got a Cancerian Ascendant when she has her Sun in this particular position?' With the kind of primal male image which is reflected in her Sun, why does she need a self-image that is symbolized by a Cancerian Ascendant? In other words, why has she chosen to see herself in this Cancerian way when she has her Sun and Moon in their respective positions?

The groundwork for this approach has already been laid down in chapter 4 when I stated that in my view the planets, and the Sun and the Moon, should be seen as a natural process of evolution each in turn being derived from the original womb-unity of the Horoscope itself as a complete, but as yet undifferentiated, entity, and indeed before that in chapter 3 when we saw the natural correlation of the heavenly bodies one to the other proceeding from unity to multiplicity.

If we bear in mind this basic frame-work then we have a natural order which forms the structure of the psyche as a dynamic, living process and we can then begin to ask why one factor has been developed in relation to the others, according to its own individual pattern. So we have seen that the Ascendant, for example, symbolizing the focus of the Persona or self-image, arises as a direct result of the original parental-images which are symbolized in the Sun and Moon. It is therefore entirely appropriate that we should ask why Alicia should see herself in this particular way, why she should have developed a Cancerian Ascendant with her particular parental-images in the Sun and Moon.

Therefore, having seen the general relationship between one factor in the Horoscope to another in chapter 4, having seen there that in all cases the Ascendant will be the way the individual reacts towards his Sun and Moon, we can now look at the particular Horoscope of the individual and ask why this particular person reacts in this particular way. We can, and should, go further than this. Although each factor in the Horoscope is derived from the original unity according to the diagram in Figure 4.1, nevertheless all the factors in the Horoscope are in some way related to all the others just because they are all parts of the whole, as we have seen in chapter 5.

It is therefore just as valid, and important, in trying to understand Alicia as a whole, and in trying to understand her mental process in particular, to ask why she should have her Mercury in Pisces making a close square aspect to Uranus when she has the other factors in her Birth Chart in their respective positions. Why does she see the world in this emotional, yet highly individualistic, manner in the context of her particular make-up, when her feelings are apparently so extrovert? These are questions which the client, in trying to realize her nature and her potentials, is asking, explicitly or implicitly. Alicia asked 'Why' on a number of occasions. Why was she always being attracted to men who appeared to be supportive but who let her down? Why specifically was she attracted to Virgoans when she had only Saturn in that Sign?

We saw in chapter 2 that the Humanist-Existentialist school places primary emphasis on the individual taking responsibility for his own life. Not only does the 'Why' approach unite the psyche but if we also ask the question in the sense of why this person has chosen to have this Ascendant in view of his Sun and Moon, we shift the responsibility towards him. Inasmuch as astrology is a way of perceiving, this shift in emphasis is a salutary one.

We need not of course press the point to its limits but rather try to redress the balance against a deterministic, materialistic viewpoint which blames outside forces alone for the individual's problems. By reorientating the responsibility back to the individual he is helped to discover within himself the ability and the freedom to live his own life. This, of course, was what the Humanist-Existentialist school was trying to achieve in swinging the pendulum away from outside circumstances which appeared to act upon an unwilling individual.

So we can ask why Alicia has her Sun in the 10th House when it is opposite Neptune. And we can answer that because she perceived her father as ineffective and has the resultant weak yang image within herself so she needs to prove herself in the world 'out there' and specifically through a career. It is therefore not a question of blaming any outside, or inside, force for the conflicts that exist within us. We do not take responsibility by blaming ourselves any more than we avoid it by blaming others. What we do is to try to understand, and in doing so, to put our lives in perspective so that we can be free to take responsibility in the present.

It is difficult to achieve this realization because it is virtually impossible to see oneself objectively and unless we learn to perceive the Horoscope in a unified way we become torn between outer and inner. The problem was brought out in the case of a young woman called Cheryl who had her Moon in Aries close to an Ascendant in the same Sign. On the face of it there was a clear paradox here. With the Moon in Aries, her feelings, which originated from the mother-image, were independent and she had a great need to express herself in her own way. But with the Moon close to her Ascendant she was tied to her mother.

The conflict that was generated by this paradox was apparent in her life. On the one hand she appeared to be assertive to the point of eccentricity. She was a fervent supporter of women's rights, adopted a combination of masculine clothes together with closely cropped hair which she had dyed in green and purple streaks. On the other hand she lived next door to her mother and had married an over-protective husband who had both his Sun and Moon in Cancer.

When we adopt the 'Why' approach we begin to get beneath the opposing characteristics and find the unifying theme. With her Moon in Aries, why did she have her Ascendant in the same Sign so close to that maternal-image? Cheryl perceived her mother according to her Moon in Aries, as someone who was outgoing, independent and strong. On an unconscious level she reacted against that image through a sense of anger because she missed a close, emotional relationship. Her appearance was a scarcely concealed attack on her mother's puritanical, traditional outlook although consciously she was quite unaware of her effect.

At the same time, just because she felt the emotional distance from her mother so keenly she needed all the more to be close to her. So, too, she was attracted to a partner who was moulded in the form of the mother she missed. But being close to her mother, and having an over-protective husband, her own individuality was threatened and she was driven to assert herself. Then, as the original mother-image through her Moon was transformed into her feminine side, the conflict manifested in her relationships with her marriage to a very 'maternal' man whom she left for long periods to 'do her own thing'. Thus she was drawn towards the very thing she was running away from but, in unconsciously reacting against it, she was also drawn to fight it. Essentially, the same anger which she felt against her mother and her husband was the anger she felt against her own femininity which came out in her aggressive appearance which she admitted her mother detested.

When she asked herself 'why?' she came to appreciate the nature of the conflict within her. She was able to see herself as an independent person in her own right and also her mother as an individual in her own right. Instead of feeling angry about her mother and her own feminine side she was able to express her real self in an independent, constructive way, using the assertive energy that was a part of her, but not against others on an unconscious level. In this way she no longer blamed others or herself and she felt able to be the mother she had run away from.

3 The Birth Chart as a continuum

> In this eternal birth wherein the Father generates the Son, the soul has flowed into the essence and the image of the God-head has been imprinted in her.

MEISTER ECKHART[3]

In this last example we have seen the way that conflict is born with the images in the Birth Chart. In this section I want to examine these conflicts in detail so that we can come to a better understanding of how the psyche operates and thus how the individual can get more in touch with himself. In coming to a true understanding of the psyche in the symbolism of the Birth Chart we need to be aware of the inner meaning of the factors as we do of the Birth Chart as a whole.

In order to do this we should begin with the fundamental question: 'What can be seen in the Birth Chart?' This question is usually taken for granted. It is assumed that we see only the character and we are then left with the paradoxes that manifest in the different sides of that character. And when we find, as is often the case, that the individual does not fulfil what is in his Horoscope in terms of character we either say that in some way he is failing to live up to his potentials or, worse still, we abandon the factors as they are in the Horoscope and search for meaning in some artificial technique.

The Birth Chart always describes a person's *needs*. Sometimes these needs will manifest as character. Sometimes a person's needs are contained within his character. In order to understand the individual's nature we must appreciate the difference between his needs and his character and the relationship that exists between them. Appreciating this difference often provides the clue to the paradox that exists within the individual. For often the conflict is the result of a need which arises from the original image in the Birth Chart. Thus we saw that Alicia's need for an identity in the world, specifically through a career, was the result of the weak father-image contained in her Sun-Neptune opposition.

The real needs are contained in the unconscious and it is the task of the therapist to enable the individual to experience these unconscious needs by bringing them out into consciousness. It is therefore a mistake to see the Horoscope purely in terms of character. It is the underlying principles that are described in the Horoscope. The unity of those principles splits and thus the conflict is born between the influence which created the image and the innate need that stems from it. Even if the need appears in a negative form, as it did in Cheryl's case, this is only because it manifests in that way unconsciously before she is enabled to use the need positively for herself.

Let us see how the conflicts within the factors themselves arise. First, the images contained in each factor are themselves ambivalent. Thus each planet, and the Sun and Moon, are Janus-faced. What Jung has termed the 'archetypes as such', the cores, have two sides. The Moon as the mother, simply by being the mother, has the archetypal duality of devotion and destruction which is the subject of myth. In the womb is encompassed the same principle as the tomb as the faces of the Moon change from the love of Mary to the terror of Hecate. Every mother, however kind, loving, giving she may be provokes in some measure the image of Kali and all who approach are in danger of being devoured. Similarly the power of the male image through the father which provides structure through its strength and order can by its very nature inhibit the development of the emerging child.

Second, there will be conflict within the image of the factor as revealed in the Birth Chart. Thus the actual parent will be ambivalent in his or her own way. We can see an example of this in Jung's Birth Chart. Jung had a close square aspect from his Moon in Taurus to Uranus and a similar aspect from his Sun in Leo to Neptune. The Moon in Taurus square Uranus describes in a relatively simple way his ambivalent mother who, according to Jung, appeared to have two personalities which she switched from one to the other. The Sun in Leo square Neptune describes his father's influence in a subtler way. On a conscious level Jung perceived his father as pleasant and kind, but unconsciously he regarded him as a failure who was unable to provide him with the strong male image he needed in order to assert himself.

Thus within the actual factor in the Birth Chart a conflict is born. There is no way of telling from the factors themselves whether the conflict is the result of the parents in an objective sense or of the child's subjective perception or a combination of the two for outer and inner merge in the images. What can be seen, and what matters, is the result in the individual's psyche. If we go back to Alicia's Sun which is in Aries in the 10th House conjunct Mars and Venus and opposite Neptune, this conflict could have been formed in a number of ways. The whole complex which forms the Sun image could have been a description of her actual father, a person who appeared to be strong but suffered from some inner weakness or defect, who had to prove himself and who was aggressive because he could not express his feelings. Alicia may then have simply taken over this image in its entirety which was translated into the complex that formed her own male, assertive side.

On the other hand the image may in part describe the father, or Alicia's way of perceiving him, as an ineffective man who could not express his real feelings, and she then developed her own need to assert her identity in the world by being someone in her own right. In this way she chose to place her Sun in Aries in the 10th House to compensate for the Neptune opposition. However the image actually came into being both sides of the conflict will manifest in the individual.

In Alicia's case because the image of her father is ineffective she will be attracted to men who are weak because that is the essential image she has of men through her Sun. At the same time, because she had this ineffective paternal-image she will look for a strong partner to bolster her own inner sense of weakness. Then the conflict arises because if she succeeded in finding someone who was really strong it would diminish her own sense of power and assertiveness which is vulnerable because of the weak Sun. So she goes round in circles because the image operates on an unconscious level and because in attracting to herself from outside that which she lacks within her she enforces the real lack. What she really needs is a partner who is supportive without destroying her own individuality or power, but being unaware of this she simply attracts partners who appear to be strong but who are in some way ineffective.

Third, there will be a conflict between the different factors in the Birth Chart. The conflict will manifest directly where the factors are pairs and indirectly because, as the model of the Tree illustrated, all the factors form a relationship with each other. Thus in some way the Sun and Moon will complement each other. Sometimes there will be clear evidence of a strong mother and weak father, for example. At other times the situation will be more subtle but at all times the way in which one parent is perceived will in itself affect the way the individual perceives the other.

Thus in Jung's Birth Chart we have seen in his Sun and Moon two figures which oppose each other. A strong, earthy, individualistic mother and an ineffective father. On the other hand we can see the images on a more subjective level. So just because he perceived his mother as ambivalent, the position of his Sun describes the way Jung needed to see his father. With the sense of separation engendered from his mother, he needed to belong to something greater than himself, he needed to be important and so he developed, or chose if we like, his Sun in Leo square Neptune. In so far as he saw himself cut off from the earth with his Moon in

Taurus square Uranus, he needed to be closer to heaven through his Sun in Leo square Neptune.

We can also turn the situation around as in Ghandi's Horoscope which is illustrated in Figure 8.1. There, with his weak male side symbolized by the unaspected Sun in Libra in the 12th House, Ghandi needed to develop a very powerful female side and thus he chose his Moon in Leo in the 10th House at the apex of both a T-Square and a Grand Trine embracing over half the planets in his Birth Chart.

Whether or not one accepts the idea of the individual choosing his or her Horoscope, this way of looking at a Birth Chart does show that both the conflicts within the individual factors and the conflicts which are apparent between the factors themselves are all derived from the same source. They are not separate parts of the psyche isolated and apart from the other parts. On the contrary they are all parts of the whole. The conflicts which arise are inevitable and natural. For whatever reason the images came into being in the first place they can always be used by the individual in a positive way.

What the individual cannot do is to get away from the factors that are within him. He can only face them and transform them and contain all of them as aspects of the whole that constitute his self. If we regard the psyche as a dynamic process whereby conflict is produced as the attempt of one side developing to balance the other, then we can see the positive value of the resultant dichotomy and the meaning behind the ostensible paradox.

CHAPTER 8
Self-realization – the process of discovery

1 *A star danced – Who am I?*

My mother cried; but then a star danced, and under that was I born.

SHAKESPEARE *Much Ado About Nothing*

Having understood how to perceive the psyche through the symbolism of the Horoscope we now need to enable the client to experience that which he is for himself. We have seen the different ways the factors in the Horoscope may manifest, we have seen that they represent the client's needs and that it is as needs that they must manifest if he is to realize his potentials; we have also seen the relationship between the various aspects of the psyche and the way that they produce conflict within the psyche.

How can the individual resolve his conflicts? How can he transform them so that their energy is used constructively? Whitmont has written:

A psychological conflict can only be dealt with by holding on, with an extreme awareness of the meanings and implications, to both sides, by suffering the crucifixion, as it were, in the pain of the conflicting opposites *without identifying* with either one .... We need not feel compelled to resolve the impasse or to do away with it.[1]

Although everyone has conflicts the nature of these varies greatly from person to person. The Birth Chart illustrated in Figure 8.1 is that of Christine and here the conflicts are brought

155

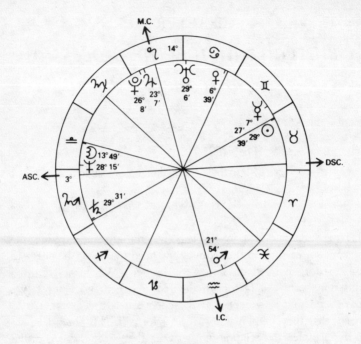

Figure 8.1   *Horoscope of Christine*

out in high relief in a pattern known as a Grand Cross where there is a series of square and opposition aspects which together interlock and bring the energies concerned very closely together.

Any such pattern produces difficulties because of the obvious conflicts which impinge one upon the other. Looking at the pattern pictorially it illustrates only too well a 'crucifixion'. The difficulties in this case are emphasized with Saturn very closely opposed to the Sun bringing out to an even greater extent the idea of 'crucifixion' in the cross of Saturn, and also in Mars and the Jupiter-Pluto conjunction being relatively close to the M.C.-I.C. axis.

Christine herself described her situation when she said that she managed to 'survive by hanging on and having faith', a remarkable reflection of Whitmont's statement. She saw her own psyche split by internal conflict. The resultant inner tension manifested with one part of her enjoying her work in local government while another was studying herbalism and astrology because she felt frustrated in her work. In addition there were conflicts in her domestic life. Her husband's activities in the animals' rights movement made her 'seize up with tension'. She felt she should have a child but was not sure. She was concerned about her 'spiritual' direction. Finally she ended up by saying that she felt as if she might explode and blow up.

It would be all too easy for Christine to identify with one or other of her different sides, not only because certain conflicts are brought out in relief through the Grand Cross, but also because that pattern in itself is one 'side' of her personality, which shows up the other in its own contrast. While the factors I have mentioned are part of a more obvious series of conflicts, through their juxtaposition, other factors, no less important, are overshadowed: notably her Moon in Libra in the 12th House which is effectively unaspected and her Venus in Cancer which is similarly unaspected.

Thus when we look at the surface of this Birth Chart we see on the one hand the ostensible conflicts which are brought out in Christine's Grand Cross, while on the other we see the unintegrated feminine side which is latent in her unaspected Moon and Venus. When we look under the surface for a unifying theme which brings the two sides together and therefore the Birth Chart as a whole, we can see in the Moon's position the detachement from her emotions which is translated through her Saturn as the fear of getting through to her deep feelings which inhibits her inner being in her Sun and which can lead to avoiding the physical and material aspect of reality with her Neptune close to her Ascendant. This in turn frustrates her assertive nature in Mars which is then projected through her husband and cuts her off from her desire for children through her Venus in Cancer.

It is inevitably difficult to accept so many different needs which appear to point in so many directions and it is therefore natural to assume that a choice must be made. Choices do of course have to be made but the assumption, natural in itself, that the choice must be through one area of one's life rather than another, and therefore between one side of one's Horoscope and another, is a false one. It is for this reason that we need to see the unity behind the multiplicity which is revealed on the surface through the parts in the different factors in the Horoscope.

If the natural tendency to choose in this way which amounts to identifying with one side is avoided, if by accepting both sides we suffer the crucifixion, then we come to realize that the opposites which manifest through the different sides amount to the same thing. For out of unity they return to unity. And Christine, by hanging on and having faith, did begin the task of resolving her conflicts. She was asked to take on more responsibility at work which centred on the administration of child abuse and so found a positive way of channelling her assertive energy in conjunction with her maternal need for children.

She decided she would take the plunge and have children and felt happy with her decision. She accepted her need to be in touch with the earth as well as her own physical side by taking an allottment and her husband also made the decision to give up his animal rights campaign when they had children. Jung made the point that if, instead of trying to force the issue and make a direct choice, the individual hangs on to both sides, then a third force will appear which resolves the conflict. Christine had shown concern about her 'spiritual' side which, with her own knowledge of astrology, she not unnaturally associated with Neptune's position near her Ascendant. She had been told that with this position she should develop her 'spiritual' nature but by separating the 'spirit' from her nature as a whole she could only enforce the conflict within her.

In getting in touch with her own nature she was asking the question which we all ask: 'Who am *I*?' Then she could ask: What does Neptune mean to *me*? That alone is what mattered to her. And in discovering where her needs lay she found that the Neptune factor was not leading her away from herself, but that on the contrary, the temptation to escape into a spiritual realm 'out there' was a negative expression of this principle. The real meaning of Neptune in her Horoscope was that the spirit lay in accepting her physical, emotional, and sexual needs which were at once contained in and blocked out by the Scorpio and Taurus factors in her Birth Chart. Then Saturn was transformed into the Sun it opposed and no longer hid its light.

If we identify with one side rather than another we fail to appreciate that both sides are aspects of the whole psyche. This realization lies at the very root of understanding the conflicts which exist within all of us and enables the individual to experience those conflicts. If we look at the Horoscope in the traditional way and regard each factor as an isolated entity then it is very difficult to avoid the effective disintegration of the personality and thus the healing process is reversed.

So if we look at Neptune in Christine's Birth Chart as someting apart from her Sun in Taurus we will say that she has physical needs or, if we look at the factors in terms of character, we will say that she is practical and sensuous because she has a Taurean Sun, and because she has Neptune rising she is also 'spiritual' or imaginative or deceptive. Now on a purely mundane level she is a mixture of these two different, and opposing, sides. But perceiving her Horoscope in that way neither helps to an understanding of who she is nor does it help her to get in touch with herself as a whole.

If on the other hand, we adopt the approach I put forward in the last chapter and ask instead: Why has she got Neptune on her Ascendant when she has her Sun in Taurus opposing Saturn? and: What is the relationship between the two sides? then we can begin to understand how the opposites are in reality attributes of the whole. Just because her physical needs are inhibited she seeks to avoid the physical and turns to the 'spiritual' instead of recognizing this 'spiritual' need, genuine in itself, as the fulfillment of the physical and material.

In this way she can be brought to appreciate what both the Taurean side and the Neptune side mean to her and by accepting both she can realize their essential unity. Hence she neither devalues her genuine idealism nor does she use it negatively by trying to avoid reality. Equally she can accept her physical side and channel it in accordance with her ideals towards a practical and humanitarian goal.

2 In the darkness – realizing the personality

Truly, it is in the darkness that one finds the light, so when we are in sorrow and distress, then this light is nearest of all to us.

MEISTER ECKHART[2]

The real choice, therefore, lies in using the factors in the Birth Chart in the right way. And this means the way that is right for the individual. But it is not a question of just consciously choosing how to use a particular factor or the Birth Chart as a whole. As Meister Eckhart, in common with all great mystics, pointed out it is only by going into the darkness and getting to the root of the conflicts which lie buried deep within the unconscious that we can find the solution and discover what is right for us.

One of the practical problems with many of the modern 'alternative' therapies and with much of the philosophy behind the Humanist-Existential school, is that the ideal of taking personal responsibility, excellent in itself, can result in the attempt to make choices simply by will power. For some patients this is indeed appropriate and in the case of such people it is right that the therapist should enter into a specific contract with them and ensure that they adhere to it.

But when the problems are deep within the unconscious then no amount of rational will power can solve them. First they must be experienced by confronting them and this often means going back to their origins, and second, it means discovering where the real conflicts lie. The difficulty in practice is that the client will be drawn in two directions simultaneously. He will be drawn away from the image that is within him because he regards it as a negative influence and therefore he reacts against it, while at the same time because it is now a part of his psyche he will inevitably be drawn towards it. So he ends up fighting himself, seeing what is now within him in other people and outside situations, and failing to recognize that it is also a part of himself. This, then, is the real conflict, not so much between one side of the personality and the other, not so much a battle between the Sun and Moon as a battle within the Sun and Moon themselves.

Because the heavenly bodies in astrology are mainly regarded as pairs – the Sun and Moon, Venus and Mars, Jupiter and Saturn, it is tempting to polarize the psyche by believing that one factor confronts its partner, thereby enforcing the archaic idea that one is good and the other bad which was inherent in the ancient concept of 'benefic' and 'malefic'. So Freud's thesis that the two most powerful urges of human beings are the creative and destructive, or libido and mortido, would on this basis correspond to Venus and Mars respectively. That, however, is a fallacy. The creative and destuctive power within each human being resides within both the Venus and the Mars principle. Each can be used creatively or destructively and neither in itself is any better or worse than the other.

The inner conflict within the factors themselves was illustrated very well by the case of Peter. Peter was a very intelligent young man who had failed to find any direction or motivation in his life. Everything came very easily to him, he was personable, had good looks, had inherited a great deal of money and yet he never managed to succeed in anything he started. He told me that at school he was lazy and anti-authoritarian but still managed to get excellent results in his 'A' levels and gained a place at University.

The conflict was illustrated here in the position of Peter's Saturn in Leo close to his Midheaven which made a square aspect to his Taurean Sun. That complex symbolizes a restrictive father-image which threatened to destroy his personal power and which affected his own identity in the world. Now on the one hand he reacted against this 'outside' influence by refusing to co-operate at school, while on the other he was drawn towards it by concentrating on scientific subjects and by applying for a very practical course in engineering.

This pattern between reacting against the inhibitive side of Saturn on the one hand, while being drawn towards its practical nature on the other was to continue throughout his life. He gave up the course in engineering and was accepted at another University to study agriculture. Then he again reacted against orthodoxy. Instead of pursuing his degree course he took a job on a farm in order to study organic farming. His next venture was to set up a business selling organic fertilizers which failed because he reacted against the practical, business side. He then literally went back to live with his father before leaving to join a commune. But he did not feel at home in the communal atmosphere, so he swung the pendulum once again and got a position as a teacher. Shortly after that his health broke down and by refusing to take orthodox medicine he almost died experimenting with various alternative techniques.

When he finally regained his health he got another job teaching only to be made redundant when the school closed down owing to financial difficulties. The pattern here is quite clear, swinging now towards and now away from the principle contained in his Saturn, now reacting against the influence that he regarded as negative because it prevented him developing his individuality and then running back again under its shadow.

Although this constant swinging from one side to the other, now towards and now away from the Saturn principle, may appear only as a negative reaction, it can also be regarded as the inevitable attempt of the psyche to come to terms with the factor within itself. In *The Integration of the Personality* Anthony Storr wrote: 'Just as all things grow, develop, and come to be whatever their inherited structure predetermines that they shall be, so a man is urged by the forces of which he is largely unconscious to express his own uniqueness, to be himself, to realise his own personality.'[3] And in order to learn the individual must make his own mistakes.

The conflicts which are within the factors in the Horoscope, the ambivalence contained within Peter's Saturn, the restrictive father-figure whch implied for him that authority was something restrictive and which therefore led him to deny his own authority because he was unable to accept it as a part of himself, are more likely to be brought out into the open when there are specific aspects between those factors and other factors in the Birth Chart. Nevertheless, we must never lose sight of the fact that it is primarily the ambivalence and conflict within the factors themselves that need to come out in the first instance.

The way the conflicts are inherent in each individual will vary depending on the position of the factors in the individual's Birth Chart. The square aspects bring the conflicts out in the highest relief as they drive the individual towards a sense of challenge and in Peter's case he was constantly driven towards meeting the problem contained in his Saturn through its square aspect to his Sun. The opposition enables the individual to face the conflict but instead of driving him towards its resolution he is more likely to project it outwards on other people and the events he attracts to himself.

With the conjunction the conflict is again shown up but here the tendency is for it to be turned inward onto the individual himself. The trine aspect, with its sense of ease, may make the conflict apparent but the individual's awareness in this case is likely to be of a theoretical nature. He may talk about his problems, even complain that he cannot do anything about them, but effectively he will try to avoid them. Where there are no aspects, and in this context I mean no close traditional aspects, the conflicts are likely to operate on an unconscious level and it will be all the more difficult to bring them into the open or to be aware of them in any way. Then they stand as it were apart and the process of integration into the whole is much more of a problem.

With these points in mind let us return to Alicia and see how her conflicts manifested. We may recall that she stated originally that she had emotional difficulties, but that she was very happy in her work. On the first occasion she described her relationships in the past and the one in which she was then involved. Of the past, she described them as 'disastrous attractions, with delusion a feature of them all, to the wrong people.' She had been married while in her twenties to a husband who was six years younger, a man who was very talented and very disturbed. They lived together for eighteen months, then split up and eighteen months later he committed suicide.

If we start by looking at the two primary images in her Horoscope – the Sun and the Moon – we can see the conflicts that exist within her, that determine her needs and the influences which produced those images. On the face of it both these bodies have a great deal in common. Both are in Aries, both oppose Neptune by about the same orb, both are close to each other in the diurnal circle although technically the Sun is in the 10th House and the Moon in the 11th in the Placidean system. However, despite the similarities, when we look at these factors in the context of the Birth Chart as a whole, as well as seeing the obvious difference in the Sun lying next to Mars and Venus, it will be clear how different they are.

Looking at Alicia's Sun in Aries in the 10th House we can see that she needs a sense of identity in the world, she needs to be successful, she needs to be her own person, to achieve in her own right. Those needs of course imply independence which in themselves imply a potential conflict with relationships. Why then does she have these needs contained in her Sun? Although her needs are strong her basic image of the male figure, through her own father, is weak, and there is a sense of anger and even violence here with the Mars conjunction. In one sense we can then see the need to be assertive as the compensation for her anger at her weak male image, which originated from her father and which is liable to be projected onto other males whom she attracts according to the same inner image.

Unconsciously she felt let down by her father, and therefore she will unconsciously expect to be let down by men. And just because of the Neptune factor, implying a sense of unreality or weakness about her father, she will try to make up for this lack by believing him to be someone particularly effective. This is why it is so difficult to admit the truth of a Neptune aspect. The very lack makes the individual compensate by believing that the person is better than they are and so they try to replace the void within themselves through their imaginings. So, too, they idealize men and will be drawn as was Alicia into relations in which 'delusion is a feature'.

Here the seeds of the conflict are born. On the one hand, lacking a strong father-figure, she has made one up according to her own image and her own imaginings. She wants a strong man to support her and therefore is attracted to men who appear to be strong, just as her own father appeared to be. But as the Neptune opposition is part of this image she will end up with someone who is really weak as her own father was. And inside her there is also the latent anger which is symbolized by Mars. Anger at being let down by the weakness which she cannot admit.

It is not easy to face the conflicts which lie within one's unconscious and how far these conflicts are latent depend very much on the individual. The more deeply they are buried the more they need to be drawn out and so it is that they will be attracted to the individual through constant forms of projection, usually in partnerships but also through the other events and situations that the individual attracts to himself throughout his life.

3 *The heaven espy – experiencing the Horoscope*

A man may look on glass
On it may stay his eye:
Or if he pleaseth, through it pass
An then the heaven espy.

GEORGE HERBERT *The Temple*

According to the American psychiatrist, Harry Stack Sullivan, we do not merely *have* experiences – we *are* our experiences. Reality is the reality that we experience. Until we experience something, it is not real for us. It means nothing to us. If is not a part of our being. Most people do not experience themselves, they live apart from themselves, they are not in touch with themselves nor are they aligned to their inner being which is symbolized by their Birth Chart.

In order to resolve the conflicts within ourselves we are driven towards them. Most people, it not all people, are driven in some way towards their conflicts, whether it be in relationships, by their actions in the world, or even through illness. But most people do not recognize the purpose of what they do, or what they believe just 'happens' to them. By seeing the person as a whole, we can enable him to realize the factors within himself and to experience in a positive way the potentials that are contained in his conflicts.

It is very difficult to see oneself directly. Although much has been said about the negative aspects of projection it is almost inevitable that we seek some kind of reflection to see ourselves. Therapy itself is such a relationship with the patient projecting his problems onto the therapist. The Birth Chart too provides a reflection whereby one can see the mirror image of the psyche.

Alicia could not accept her feelings about herself or the men she attracted. She described her father as 'positive, optimistic, a wonderful person, very well thought of.' Of couse he may well have been like this on the surface and he may genuinely have been a very kind man. Nevertheless, the real situation which manifested in Alicia's unconscious is clear from the Sun image in her Birth Chart and it was this which she projected onto the men that she attracted in her life.

When she first approached me she said that things were much better in her relationships. She was now very happy with a man who seemed ideal for her and whom she had met two-and-a-half years ago. During that time she was 'happier and more content than ever before'. She went on to say that he was a wonderful lover and the relationship was mutually supportive, unlike her previous involvement when she propped up her partner.

However, when we look at this man's Birth Chart we see someone who appeared to be very outgoing and friendly with his Sun in Sagittarius, and who appeared to be highly efficient with his Ascendant in Virgo. But we then find the difficulties he had in expressing his feelings with his Moon in Virgo in the 12th House and above all with Neptune very close to his Ascendant the same sense of unreality and need for support that pervaded her own male image.

Having started with these highly positive statements, she went on to mention some problems. The first was that he was 'very committed to his work' so she did not see him as often as she would have liked. The second was that he was married to a semi-invalid wife and had two children. The third was that he appeared to have an aversion to discussing the future. In spite of these obvious drawbacks she was certain that they would have a very happy relationship together. She concluded with the remark: 'In all ways he is a very honest person.'

When the relationship finally broke down Alicia was distraught and not surprisingly felt very bitter. Charles had told her that he did not want a close and committed relationship though he wanted to remain a friend. In her fury Alicia telephoned his wife only to be told that everything Charles said was bound to be a lie.

Once again we see someone driven to resolve the conflicts within a particular complex in the Birth Chart. The Sun complex is of course only a part of the whole. In particular it is complemented by the Moon image. The Moon itself is also in Aries opposite Neptune. Once again there is a sense of unreality about this image, a failure to get the close emotional, and above all, physical sense of bonding that she needed as a child, of hands reaching out into the void and meeting – nothing.

So her own feelings are unreal and she is driven to assert them all the more to try to make up for their unreality by almost forcing them onto others in her blind impetuosity, desperately wanting love. We can see the lack of physical proximity in the lack of Earth in her Birth Chart, Saturn emphasizing rather than making up for this lack for it represents her fear, and the fear in her case is of physical intimacy, of being able to give and receive on a one-to-one, adult basis where there is equality and trust on both sides.

So what does she do? Lacking the mother she wanted, she becomes the mother herself and chooses a Cancerian Ascendant. The other face of this self-image is that the only way to be acceptable to her parents was to behave like a child. The result is that in her partnerships we find a child-parent relationship. Consciously she wants support, the support of a child from a parent, but with her lack of inner confidence through her Sun and her misgivings about her own feelings through her Moon she cannot accept the support she consciously desires.

She therefore tends to mother her partners and this in itself can be a way of avoiding a real relationship. First of all it increases the likelihood of attracting a 'child' or someone dependent. Second, it can avoid the problem of accepting a partner's love on equal terms for the mother does not expect a sharing relationship. Being afraid of losing herself if she gives of her deepest emotions she solves the problem by being attracted to someone who appears to be strong and supportive but who in fact needs support, and who appears to be capable of a real relationship but who in some way is tied down elsewhere.

The conflicts in Alicia's Birth Chart were brought out clearly in the people that she attracted and her own failure to see them as they were. She said that she had always been attracted to Virgoans although she found them asexual without realizing that that was precisely why she was attracted to them. With her Saturn in Virgo she was afraid of physical intimacy, so she found men who had their Moon in the same position as her Saturn. At first they were attracted by her strength but then they were effectively prevented from expressing their feelings as they had projected their own conflicts onto her.

Alicia started off, as many people do, by thinking there was a choice between her career and her need for relationships and that was where her conflict lay. As she progressed through our sessions and her life she came to realize that the conflicts were part of her nature as a whole. And that while she was outwardly successful in her career even that did not bring her the fulfillment she had originally believed.

Alicia was driven to use the energies that were within her. She was driven to meet them. This is the vital first step. And she did experience a great deal of what was within her. She experienced her Sun in her career and she was driven to experience it through the male image in relationships. She managed to experience her Mars in her career where she was successful, if not as happy as she first made out. In her relationships her inability to accept her need for physical contact was complicated because of her fear of intimacy. She used the Neptune factor partly through her idealism which came out in her work but she failed to a great extent to accept herself and others as they really were.

Her feelings manifested self-defensively in her Cancerian Ascendant because, with her Neptune opposite her Sun and Moon, she unconsciously felt a sense of inner weakness and a lack of reality where her feelings and her assertive needs were concerned. Thus she was afraid of giving herself in an intimate way with her Saturn in Virgo because she felt, unconsciously, that in giving herself she would lose herself. Being afraid to lose her identity with the centre of her inner being, her Sun, opposite Neptune, she was even more afraid of accepting love from others and so she attracted 'asexual' men through her shadow area – the Saturn in Virgo.

Once the factors are brought out into the open the client is then forced to work through them. And by working through them he arrives at the point where the natural dynamism of the psyche takes over and the opposites turn into each other. This is why it is important to recognize the underlying principle in the factors within the Horoscope. By the actual work of going into these factors realization comes about and they are made a part of the individual.

In the same way by facing the Saturn-Sun square in Peter's Horoscope the principle of authority, Saturn, is eventually turned into his own power, his Sun, and transformation takes place. Then he is no longer constantly drawn towards authority in some outside guise but he realizes it as a part of his own being. This is the meaning of transformation as opposed to sublimation, for in the former case the drive within the factor is changed while in the latter it is directed elsewhere and the problem is not solved on an inner level.

4 *Suffering the cruciufixion – containment and perfection*

    How else but through a broken heart
    May Lord Christ enter in.
                            OSCAR WILDE *The Ballad of Reading Gaol*

Earlier in this book I compared the psyche to the Grail and the task of the individual searching for self-realization to the king seeking the Grail. The Birth Chart is the Kingdom. The individual is the King. To change the barren waste land of his kingdom into fertile ground he needs to recognize what is within him. All too often astrologers never find the spirit they are seeking in the Birth Chart simply because they fail to recognize it when they see it. The spirit is the Horoscope as a whole and the whole of the Horoscope. Wholeness, the healing process which is the aim of therapy of whatever kind, lies in accepting and experiencing every part of the whole and in recognizing that in relating as a whole we find our spirit. In the words of Edward Edinger: 'To be related to one's individuality means to accept all that is encountered within us as meaningful and significant aspects of the whole.'[4]

The ancient Egyptians believed that when the deceased entered the judgment hall of the Dead he or she must address each of the forty-two gods and state that he had not offended the attribute of the Godhead represented by that deity. The Horoscope is our personal representation of every attribute of the Godhead contained in its unity in our individual spirits and it is this pattern that must be accepted in its entirety.

Because the original unity, the spirit in its undifferentiated form, splits into different sides conflict is brought into being, one side opposes the other. Part of the difficulty of accepting ourselves as a whole is because we have been conditioned to believe that if there are two sides one must be right and the other wrong, and part is because of the inherent ambivalence which is within the factors in the Birth Chart. Because of the ambivalent maternal-image in Alicia's Horoscope, with Neptune opposite her Moon, she cannot accept her need to give of her feminine side and therefore she projects this need negatively in relationships and suffers deception and attracts men who seek emotional support from her. And she reacts against this image with her Cancerian Ascendant. Then with these two very different sides, the Arien and the Cancerian, she naturally assumes she has to make a choice between them.

But although the Cancerian and the Arien are two separate sides of her nature they are still both aspects of her being as a whole. She cannot get rid of one and just live according to the other. Nor is it a question of one being wrong and the other right. Every factor within her is a valid and necessary part of her. The choice therefore lies not between one side and another but within the sides themselves. First by transforming those sides so that their positive potential comes out and second, by integrating them into a whole.

So, for whatever reason these two sides came into being, they are now parts of her nature. She does genuinely need both emotional security with her Cancerian Ascendant and she needs to assert herself and find her identity as a person with her Arien side. The important thing is to appreciate that both sides sprung from one source and that in order to be whole she must reconcile them so that they once again reflect her nature as a whole. Thus rather than trying to choose between career and relationships, she needs to recognize her need for achievement, independence, idealism and caring in her career, and also in relationshiips her need both to assert herself and to care and be cared for.

In order to achieve this end the individual can only work through the various aspects of his being and in this way suffer the crucifixion. In the words of Jacobi: 'The meaning and purpose of a problem seems to lie not in its solution but in our working through at it incessantly.'[5] Problems are never really solved in any final sense. Life means living, balancing the different sides and constantly working through them. It means facing the anger, the bitterness, the hatred for what they are. If the individual is unable to face the fear and the violence that lie in his psyche then he will repress or devalue those principles which lie within him.

Then they inevitably have to find another outlet, and are either projected onto other people or are turned inwards on the individual himself. We saw in Figure 1.1 that Rosalind felt a sense of inhibition which affected both the assertive power of her Sun and the emotional feelings of her Moon with Saturn contacting both these bodies. She felt a great sense of duty which prevented her from expressing herself naturally and spontaneously. We can see the emphasis here on the physical and material aspect of life and on the inhibition which affected her giving herself on an intimate, physical level with her Saturn in Virgo. In particular the physical side of her nature was blocked with Mars in Taurus in the 12th House square Pluto, a very close aspect, and also her feelings were inhibited with Saturn opposing her Moon in Pisces.

Instead of facing the physical side of her nature she sought meaning inside herself and developed what she called an interest in 'the spiritual side of life'. The result in her particular case was not to project her conflicts onto others as she was genuinely and in all humility searching for the truth but rather onto herself. Consequently she developed back problems and her joints seized up although she was only thirty-four when she sought help. What she needed to do was to reconcile the Piscean need for the 'spiritual' in a practical, physical way and soon after she came for advice she began a course in homeopathy which not only resulted in her own cure on a physical level but which in her words was 'of real use to the world'.

The other reason for believing that one side of our personality must be good and the other bad is because we have been conditioned in our society in the belief that a part of our nature is inherently evil. Therefore, because we cannot accept this 'evil' side, which in Jungian terms is the Shadow, we project it onto others. So instead of accepting ourselves as we are and trying to transform what is within us we try to escape from our real nature and search for the 'spirit' outside. Thus we end up alienated from our own nature and from our own spirit. The point of transformation is to accept the energies that exist within us, which are fixed constants, and to effect an inner change.

All the energies in the Horoscope can be used in a positive way. All, taken together and integrated, form the whole person. The aim is not perfection, returning to the undifferentiated state of unity, but containment in accepting and balancing the conflicts which comprise the spirit of the individual. If we hang on to both sides and work through them then we can resolve them into the state of balance that enables us to be aligned with our essence or spirit. The way is not easy and as we have seen the goal is never achieved in any final sense. Gandhi was one who I think went as far as anyone to achieve a state of balance. His Birth Chart is illustrated in Figure 8.2.

This Birth Chart is a good example of someone affecting a very real and wonderful transformation, whence the spirit in all its beauty shone through a very human and fallible man. We can see here both the conflicts which were drawn out into the open through the hard aspects, especially in the close T-Square linking Gandhi's Moon in Leo in the 10th House with Venus and Mars in close conjunction in Scorpio in the 1st House on the one side and another close conjunction between Jupiter and Pluto in Taurus in the 7th House on the other.

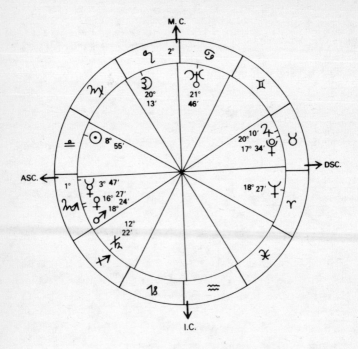

Figure 8.2 *Horoscope of Mahatma Gandhi*

And we can see the other kind of problem with the unaspected Sun in Libra in the 12th House. In addition there is the Grand Trine linking his Moon with Saturn and Neptune, and Mercury close to his Scorpio Ascendant, Mercury being otherwise unaspected. Gandhi's life was a continual struggle to find himself, not only within himself but even more in the world outside, and to his dying day when he was assassinated because of the contentions between the Moslems and Hindus that he tried to assuage, he was involved in bitter controversy.

Gandhi was always filled with self-doubts and never thought of himself as being a particularly good or saintly man. Indeed he always took pains to declare the negative side of his character, and his relations with his own children were hardly an unmitigated success, with the eldest dying a premature death, an embittered alcoholic who hated his father and all that he stood for because Gandhi had insisted on endowing him with his own high standards, although he was noticeably tolerant of other people's failings.

As a child Gandhi was so timid he could not bear to talk to anyone and in spite of his barrister's training in England and his constant public speaking he never managed to make an impression by his presence or his address. Indeed he was always to remain remarkably ordinary, even insignificant so far as appearance was concerned – until he began to talk and his inner spirit became apparent.

He remained guilty about his sexual lust and blamed himself because he had been with his child wife when his father was dying. The complexes were certainly brought out in his life. His appetite for food and sex, his vanity and anger constantly rose before him and he continually worked on them as well as sublimating them to some extent in his work. As he said: 'Man can change his temperament, can control it ... he cannot eradicate it. God gave him no such liberty.'

He did not run away from his problems or his nature. This was true not only with the obvious conflicts which are apparent in the hard aspects but also, and this is really where his greatness lay as a human being, in the ones which were latent – in the Sun, so potentially unintegrated. H.N. Brailsford remarked that Gandhi's female tendencies were at least as strong in his mental make-up as his male, and these he used in his humanitarian work and in his nursing. He met the conflicts in his appetites and sexual needs full on by taking a vow of celibacy in 1906, although they never entirely left him even in old age. He acted out his assertive needs and transformed them by fighting for peace and for his beliefs, sometimes literally in South Africa when he took part in the Boer War and in the Zulu 'rebellion', and in his non-co-operation against the British rule in India.

In addition he did not run away from his Libran Sun. He was never afraid of compromise and constantly changed his mind and actions to suit the particular circumstances of a situation even when it meant antagonising his own followers who lost face, as when he helped the British in South Africa. Gandhi always believed that man must act out his beliefs, and his primary belief was for justice. This for him entailed toleration and conciliation and fairness for both sides. The principle of arbitration was essential to his philosophy, and his life was an attempt to establish harmony between words, beliefs and acts.

In living up to these ideals Gandhi transformed and reconciled the energies within him. Although the storms continued to rage, and although he had to work on his conflicts to the end, he ceased to be troubled by them and he used the power of his complexes positively. At his funeral Sir Stafford Cripps said: 'I know of no other man of any time or indeed in recent history who so forcefully and convincingly demonstrated the power of spirit over material things.' Gandhi himself said: 'There is an indissoluble marriage between matter and spirit .... The connection between cosmic phenomena and human behaviour is a living faith which draws me nearer to God.'[6]

We, as human beings, live in the world. It is a world of which we are an integral part just as each part of our psyches is an integral part of our being. By living *our* lives, in their entirety, by accepting all that is within us and realizing its potential we find our spirit. The realization of this spirit in the flesh means the constant experience through the work which the ancient alchemists pursued. The paradox was appreciated by Gerard Manley Hopkins when he wrote: 'Man's spirit will be flesh-bound when found at best, but uncumbered.'

CHAPTER 9

A little lower than the angels –
the paradox of T.E. Lawrence

What is man that thou art mindful of him? ... Thou
madest him a little lower than the angels; thou
crownest him with glory and honour, and didst set him
over the works of thy hands.

HEBREWS 2:6

In this chapter I am going to look at a historical figure to see how
the theories I have discussed relate to a well-known individual.
The case of T.E. Lawrence is of peculiar fascination for two
reasons. First, because of the sharp contrast between two sides of
his character, the egotistical visionary who succeeded in imposing
his dreams on an alien people and who created the myth that has
survived to this day. And the sensitive, boyish figure who sought
to escape from the world by changing his name and losing himself
in the ranks.

Second, because as a great leader of men he was unique. The
age in which he was born threw up a series of great leaders, most
them born under the great conjunction of Pluto and Neptune:
Adolf Hitler, Francisco Franco, Charles de Gaulle, Josip Tito,
Benito Mussolini. The private lives of these men were subsumed
in their public role. With Lawrence it was different. The private
life intrudes on the public, tears itself, wounds what it has created.
The hero remains – but the inner soul is tortured.

If we look at the Birth Chart of Lawrence we can see the
interweaving of the public and the private. The great Neptune-
Pluto conjunction is not only intimately bound up in a T-Square
with the Moon and Venus, but, and it is here that Lawrence is

different from the other leaders, it lies very close to his Ascendant. Here we can see the confluence of inner and outer, so that his world becomes our world.

The fascination of Lawrence as a person is heightened by a number of other factors. First, his qualities were mixed. Not only was he a leader of men who made his name as a man of action, but he was also extremely intelligent, a fellow of All Souls, translator of *The Odyssey*, as well as being an excellent mechanic and with the makings of an outstanding archaeologist. Second, he had a rare insight into his own mind that few men of action, indeed few men of any kind, have shared. His great creative work, *Seven Pillars of Wisdom*, is as much a tribute to his understanding of his own psyche as a work of literature.

Lawrence lived very much in the present and yet he was bound to his past, to the unfinished business he never managed to resolve. He achieved the height of success and fame at an early age and was then driven to face his personal conflicts. Let us begin by seeing how Lawrence's character and conflicts were moulded by his parents. The father-image is contained first in the Sun's position in Leo in the 4th House making only one close aspect – a square to Jupiter. The secondary attributes of the paternal image, Saturn and Mars, are in close square aspect to each other. The contrast between the primary and the secondary illustrates beautifully the way that an influence can affect a person on an unconscious level.

On the one hand we have a very positive, but remote figure. Someone who sees or needs to see his father as a great man, someone of importance, someone special, and who in turn was encouraged to be someone out of the ordinary. But this greatness, in father and son, was not really a part of their nature. Rather it had to be grasped out of the air and imposed upon them both. And the result can be seen in the secondary attributes – Saturn in Leo square Mars in Scorpio – a blockage of the real power of Lawrence as an individual which prevented him from expressing his assertiveness. Consciously he saw his father as a hero –

unconsciously he was powerless.

The maternal-image involves the primary symbol of the Moon and also its secondary attribute, Venus, in its pattern harnessing it to the whirlwind of the generation influence embodied in the Pluto-Neptune conjunction on Lawrence's Ascendant. This womb-image bound Lawrence in its grip throughout his troubled life, creating and destroying him. He sought to escape in the desert – and founded the legend that outshone the man who sought solace in its peace.

Lawrence created an image of his father that was heroic and romantic. Thomas Robert Tighe Chapman, Lawrence's father, epitomised the Irish country gentleman. Heir to a baronetcy which he finally inherited only five years before his death, he lived with his first wife on a prosperous Irish estate – Kilna Castle in County Westmeath. The elder Thomas is described as being morose and ineffective in Ireland. He drank a good deal but was obliged to hide his drink from his intolerant wife. Edith Sarah Hamilton, who was Thomas's cousin, was described as severe, sour and religiously strict – nicknamed the 'Vinegar Queen' by the locals. The couple bore four daughters and Thomas brought over a young girl, also named Sarah, from Scotland to be a companion and governess for the children. Shortly after her engagement Thomas eloped with Sarah, leaving Edith with the children.

As Lawrence lacked a strong male image he was driven to create one, and at least he had something upon which to build, for not only was his father heir to a baronetcy but there was some distant family connection with Sir Walter Raleigh. In later life Lawrence wrote: 'My father, middle-aged, was his (Raleigh's) walking image.'[1] And he paints this picture of his father: 'On the large scale, tolerant, experienced, grand, rash, humoursome, skilled to speak, and naturally lord-like. He had been 35 years in the large life, and a spend-thrift, a sportsman and a hard rider and drinker.'[2]

It is difficult for a child to meet the expectations, or even to live up to the characters, of his parents. The square aspect that Jupiter makes to Lawrence's Sun could, in itself, have driven him to emulate a father who was truly 'lord-like' and the Saturn-Mars square could then be seen as the difficulty in living up to this image. But the remoteness of the Sun, making no other relevant contacts, and also being buried at the nadir of the Birth Chart, shows that Lawrence was not only trying to emulate a father, but a father who did not exist in the mould that his famous son had cast him.

While it is difficult to live up to a great father, it is impossible to live up to a great father who is a creation of one's own imagination. Certainly Thomas Chapman appears to have been kind and gentle, and perhaps he would have liked to have been one of the lords of life. But in fact he was totally dominated by his wives. For, like many people who are unhappy in their relationships, Thomas managed to break away from one partner only to find her mirror-image.

Always shy and unsure of himself Thomas gave up drinking when he lived with Sarah and he had no opportunity in their staightened circumstances to enjoy the hunting and shooting he had delighted in as an enthusiastic sportsman. Having eloped with a woman who was socially beneath him he was cut off from his old way of life and appears to have shrunk into himself as the family moved around the country changing their name until they settled in Oxford.

His neighbours described him as tall, gentle, sensitive and quiet. In looks and manner he retained his aristocratic heritage. It was perhaps here that Lawrence felt the difference between them which was a factor in his paternal emulation, for Lawrence himself was short, boyish and physically unremarkable. Indeed, having made the comparison of his father to Raleigh, he ends rather poignantly: 'I'm not like that side of the family though.'

Lawrence blamed his mother for the apparent change in his father. His father, once a hero, had been remodelled by his partner into a little, domestic man. Like Ouranos, lord of Heaven, he had been castrated by his wife and brought down to the realm of earth. Certainly it was around his mother that Lawrence's conflicts were centred. Sarah was clearly a remarkable woman. She was attractive, strong-willed and highly capable, efficient and energetic. She also possessed unusual energy, great charm and a prodigious will and determination.

Physically she resembled her son with her short stature and piercing china-blue eyes. Like Edith she was straightlaced, stoical and puritanical and, lacking other female models, we can see the combination of the fiery extrovert side in Lawrence's Moon in Sagittarius with the puritanical nature in his Venus in Virgo. The image of power, of domination, the archetypal Kali figure is inherent in the Pluto contact that opposes the Moon, squares Venus and lies close to Lawrence's Ascendant. Here we can see the intense struggle to grow as a separate person despite his mother's overpowering personality. 'Mother is rather wonderful:' he was to write, 'but very exciting. She is so set, so assured in mind ... I have a terror of her knowing anything about my feelings, or convictions, or way of life. If she knew they would be damaged, violated, no longer mine. You see she would not hesitate to understand them: and I do not understand them, and do not want to.'[3] Of his father, he continues 'she kept him as her trophy of power.'

The desperate struggle to be himself is apparent: 'I always felt that she was laying seige to me, and would conquer, if I left a chink unguarded.'[4] And later: 'I'm afraid of letting her get ever so little inside the circle of my integrity, and she is always hammering and sapping to get in.'[5] He also recognizes the attraction that is the other face of his fear: 'Probably she is exactly like me; otherwise we wouldn't so hanker after one another, whenever we are wise enough to keep apart.'[6]

The ambivalence that arises from the Moon-Pluto contact is one that threatens the power of the individual while at the same time making him need that power. It is clear that Lawrence was driven not only to try to break away from this influence but also that he was attracted by it. That in itself is not an insoluble problem. It may, in some cases, continue to be a problem in relationships which to some extent may be worked through. In the case of Henry II, for example, who shared both the Moon-Pluto contact, this time as a square aspect, and a Sun-Jupiter contact, he married a woman very much in the mould of his strong mother, the Empress Matilda, and had continuing problems with his associations, but he still managed to live his own life, even though it meant keeping his Queen, Eleanor of Aquitaine, a virtual prisoner.

Lawrence's mother was too close, not only emotionally, but also physically and his feelings as a whole were impregnated with her personality. Sarah, in eloping with a weak man, tried to make up for Thomas's ineffectiveness by living through her son and this naturally created great pressure on Lawrence. The situation was made increasingly difficult because of the contact that Lawrence's Moon makes with Neptune and the inclusion of Venus in this pattern. The presence of Neptune adds deceit to power. Sarah's life, in her eyes and in the eyes of her son, was a lie. On the surface she was a conventional, strict, religious mother and so, as a person, she was. Under the surface she was a fraud. She herself was illegitimate. She had taken a man away from his wife and his four children and she spent the rest of her life in sin as Edith refused to divorce Thomas.

Thus her own five children were also illegitimate. Even T.E.'s name was not his own and both parents lived in fear that their children and their neighbours would discover their secret. It may have been that other people would not have felt the problem to the extent that Sarah did, even in the moral climate of Victorian England. But with her strong sense of right and wrong, with her genuine religious convictions, her way of life meant a terrible moral conflict which made her whole existence a lie.

It has been said that Lawrence was brought up in a happy, normal background. Certainly this is true on the surface. His father took great interest in the children and enjoyed playing with them, and his mother did her best to bring them up according to her beliefs. But there can be no doubt that the truth was deliberately hidden from them with an intensity that affected the children in a very personal way as we can see from the obsessive nature of Pluto on Lawrence's Ascendant and the deceitful way that Neptune affected him in the same area. It was partly for this reason that Lawrence was to become so obsessive about the truth and why, in lacking a real world, he had to make one up for himself.

According to Lawrence's brother Arnold, their mother tried to redeem herself vicariously through her sons, to whom she transmitted her sense of sin. She wanted them to be missionaries and devote their lives to God. Lawrence was singled out especially as the one who would wash away his mother's sins, it was he who would redeem her by his own special achievements, by being an exceptional person who accomplished great deeds, preferably of a religious nature, imbued with a heroic theme.

It was also his mother who administered physical discipline in the family and here, so far as Lawrence was concerned, it was not normal chastisement, but severe whippings to the buttocks with the intention, according to Arnold, of trying to break T.E.'s will. Certainly one can see the confusion in the maternal image with this physical bonding which produced a feeling of pleasure, pain and shame blended into one and which later was to erupt into the open.

The Neptune influence made Lawrence feel that he too was deceitful. Having to deceive his friends about his illegitimacy, he felt isolated. The Pluto influence was both a source of strength and a challenge. In trying to maintain his own integrity and avoid being devoured by his mother's powerful personality, he tried to keep his distance from her as much as possible. In identifying with that image, he came to possess empathy and nurturing qualities, while at the same time these 'motherly' qualities which he introjected made him confused about his sexual identity and ensured that he was vulnerable to masochism because of his identification with his passive feminine side.

Although the obvious conflicts can be traced directly to his mother, as is apparent from the personal image which he provided for himself in the Pluto-Neptune conjunction on his Ascendant, the development of his personality was in answer to the influences of both parents. Certainly both parents shared the characteristics which led to their famous offspring's confusion as well as his greatness. Both believed they were living in sin and were worried lest the chidren discovered that they were not married. Both possessed martyr qualities. And although Lawrence placed his father on a pedestal, nevertheless his deeply ambivalent attitude clearly manifested against both parents. As he was to write:

> She did not know that the inner conflict, which made me a standing civil war, is the inevitable issue of the discordant natures of herself and my father, and the inflammation of strength and weakness which followed the uprooting of their lives and principles. They should not have borne children.[7]

Consequently the paradoxes appeared in Lawrence's nature. He identified with his parents' ideals and also with their failure to live up to them. With Saturn in Leo, his deepest fears, his Shadow, was centred on his own power but because that power was bound up with his father's powerlessness and the power of his mother which threatened him, he was unable to face it in himself and looked outside. Thus not only his feelings but the inner strength of his own being, were repressed.

Lacking reality, Lawrence idealized. Like Jung, with Neptune making an important contact to a personal point, Lawrence dreamed. Like Jung, too, he made his dreams come true and in this way both were great and remarkable people. The difference is that Lawrence's dreams were not *his* dreams and so, when by a supreme effort of will, he realized them, he felt cheated and he felt that in realizing them, he had cheated, and they crumbled into the dust of the desert.

Lawrence developed a great interest, shared by his father, in the romantic ideals of the crusaders. From 1905 to 1908 he travelled in England and France visiting the important medieval castles and his degree thesis on the military architecture of the crusades earned him a 'brilliant' first class degree at Oxford which led his tutor to take the exceptional step of giving a dinner to the examiners to celebrate it.

These dreams of an idealized period in history when women were worshipped in a ritualized and platonic fashion, and when men were heroes was to mould his later vision. His personal ideal was to be self-sufficient and austere. His power was a power not only over others as an inspired leader but over himself, the power of Pluto that he built up to defend himself against his mother's influence and the tremendous self-control, will-power and mental discipline that kept his feelings in check and channelled them towards his dreams, which is apparent in the square aspect from his Mars in Scorpio to his Saturn-Mercury conjunction in Leo. His idealism was also based on renunciation, a need to sacrifice himself for his sense of sin which is so apparent in the Neptune contact. It was this that attracted him so much to the Bedouins on his first trip to the Middle East.

The combination of power and self-abnegation was remarkable in Lawrence. On the one hand he had an overwhelming desire to impose his heroic ideals on others, while on the other he had the masochistic streak that stemmed from guilt and shame which drove him to destroy the fruits of his own desires. What makes Lawrence so different from other men is that, with the Pluto-Neptune conjunction on his Ascendant, these two opposing and conflicting drives were constantly being played out against each other on the surface of his personality.

Lawrence was at once driven to achievement, to be recognized as a hero, and then driven to punish himself for his needs. His capacity for hard work and endurance were legendary, instilled by a constant need to prove himself and to be better than others. In the words of Lieutenant Colonel Stirling: '... he could do everything and endure everything just a little better than the Arabs themselves.'[8] Although he was physically small he prided himself on his strength and courage. In his own words: 'In 1914 I was a pocket Hercules, as muscularly strong as people twice my size, and more enduring than most.'[9]

At the same time his feelings against authority, the result of his negative paternal-image, were apparent in his deliberately scruffy, unmilitary appearance as well as his antipathy towards accepted rank and honours. Although General Wingate stated that he deserved the VC for his secret and dangerous mission to Baalbeck and Damascus in 1917, Lawrence said: '(I) will never wear one or allow one to be conferred on me openly.'

The need to prove himself was apparent in his ideals as he makes clear in this passage:

> I wanted to feel what it was like to be the mainspring of
> a national movement, and to have some millions of people
> expressing themselves through me: and being a half-poet, I
> don't value material things much. Sensation and mind seem
> to me much greater, and the ideal, such a thing as
> impulse that took us into Damascus, the only thing worth
> doing.[10]

But the conflict was heightened by the dream. For, in trying to impose his vision upon the Arabs, he felt he was exploiting them and his innate feelings of deception came once more to the fore. Thus in helping the Arabs, and in identifying with their needs, and in the process imposing his ideals upon them he felt he was serving his own psychological needs and so was using them. And here too a situation which was latent within him was brought out by the actual circumstances. For Lawrence knew that the English and French were not going to honour their promise to the Arabs and give them their own country.

Lawrence was an almost classic example of sublimation rather than transformation. The Neptune factor in his Birth Chart was in a way one of his greatest strengths. Few men have ever made their dreams come true in the way that Lawrence did. Many men may dream of carving out a kingdom for a people in a distant land, or fighting like the knights of old, of being a hero. To actually bring about such a dream and make it a personal reality was something very remarkable, especially when we consider that Lawrence was no more than a junior officer in his twenties at the time.

But this idealistic vision produced an insistence on personal perfection and so provided a false image which he could never hope to realize. We can see the conflict within the factor of Neptune itself. He had to be perfect; when he was young he worked incessantly on his mind and his body to become in his words a 'perfect instrument' of some great ideal. And yet he knew that this image of perfection was a lie, that he was tainted by sin, that he was not the person he pretended to be, and in inevitably failing to live up to his image of perfection he felt more guilty than every.

We saw that Alicia, with her Moon opposite Neptune, could not accept her own feelings, she could not accept that they were real. But that made her try to relate to others all the more. Lawrence shut himself off completely from his feelings. He built a wall around them which appeared to be impregnable. He sublimated them into his vision, into his creative writing, into his ideals, into his kindness for those in need, but he could never accept them within himself nor accept feelings from others.

When his brother Frank was killed in France during the War in 1915 he found the sight of his mother giving way to grief intolerable. 'If you only knew,' he wrote to her, 'that if one thinks deeply about anything one would rather die than say anything about it.' Not for him was the catharsis of expressing his emotions; the relief of grief was repugnant to his soul.

The trouble with repressing the feelings is that they become even more powerful under the surface, waiting to break through like the molten lava in a volcano. Lawrence, with the austerity of a monk, may have succeeded in taming the dragon within like many of the great saints who were also troubled by sexual temptation. Unfortunately for Lawrence one incident was to bring this conflict out into the open without resolving it.

In November 1917 he was captured by the Turks and assaulted at Der'a by Hajim Bay, the local governor who was an ardent paederast. The details of this incident are shrouded in mystery, not least because Lawrence's own accounts vary considerably. Whether he was sexually assaulted, and if so, to what degree, he was certainly beaten, probably whipped and perhaps tortured. Whatever the reality of the situation, the incident brought out his latent conflicts and so far as his subjective feelings were concerned, the results were that he suffered physical and psychological humiliation, and moreover, that he encountered a mixture of enjoyment and degradation, the former making him feel more guilty than ever. In addition, the sexual element he felt in the assault brought out and threatened the defences he had built up during his life so far.

In itself the incident might, once the immediate traumatic effects had worn off, have led to a reconciliation of his conflicts. Unfortunately the reverse was the case and for the rest of his life he felt, in continuing to shut off his feelings, more ashamed but even more attracted to humiliation and suffering. He describes his feelings thus: 'The breaking of the spirit by that frenzied nerve-shattering pain which had degraded me to beast level when it made me grovel to it.'[11] And the result as 'a delicious warmth, probably sexual, was swelling through me.'[12] It was this that he relived in terrible nightmares for the rest of his life and which gave him the need for continual acts of penance.

Then the opposite side, the self-control that he had built up so strenuously, also came to the surface and the Saturn-Mars contact and the grip of his Pluto on his Ascendant burst out in naked violence. In September 1918 Lawrence lost control of himself and ordered the massacre of Turkish prisoners after the Turks had butchered the Arabs. Once again the details of this incident are unclear. There is no doubt that the Turks had committed atrocities against the Arabs, bayoneting children in their mothers' arms.

Some witnesses stated that Lawrence did his best to restrain the Arabs from taking revenge, others that he was not in any case in control of the Arabs, while others have blamed him for the incident. Whatever the objective truth, Lawrence, as in the Der'a episode, blamed himself and he suffered greatly as a consequence for his loss of control. '... anyone who pushed through to success,' he was to write later, 'a rebellion of the weak against their masters must come out of it so stained in estimation that afterwards nothing in the world would make him feel clean.'[13]

The combined effect of these two incidents has been summed up by one biographer, as touching off 'in an abrupt and devastating way, forbidden or unacceptable sexual, aggressive and vengeful impulses ... what he had felt as merely a strong attraction to renunciation and self-denial, a kind of idealising puritanism ... became exaggerated into a powerful need for penance through degradation and humiliation, a need that was accompanied by a permanently lowered self-regard.'[14]

The legend of 'Lawrence of Arabia' was built up after the war. Although there have been differences of opinion about his achievements, there can be little doubt that his work in Arabia was remarkable. Perhaps this work is best summed up by the military historian, Basil Liddell Hart, when he wrote: 'Allenby could not have defeated the Turks without Lawrence.'[15] Immediately after the war Lawrence continued his work for the Arab cause. Thereafter he tried to dedicate his life to the principles of service and self-sacrifice. In his life after the war we can see once again the paradox between his need for acceptance and his inability to accept himself.

The result was the creation of the myth of 'Lawrence of Arabia', a hero like the crusaders of old, while Lawrence himself tried to hide from the world. It has been suggested that he simply wanted to get away after his exertions in the war which left him worn out and depleted. But this simplistic view is not borne out by the facts. First, he worked for some years after the war with Churchill at the Peace Conference in Paris where it was his voice that gave Feisal a seat at the Conference. Second, he actively participated with Lowell Thomas in the latter's shows in 1919 which began the legend that was to surround him. Third, in writing his own story of his work with the Arabs he partly created and partly perpetuated his own myth. Fourth, in June 1920 he was elected a fellow of All Souls and if he had simply wanted to get away in a cloistered atmosphere he could hardly have found a more appropriate place.

It is clear that he wanted, not just to get away, but to punish himself, even to obliterate his personality. That the heroic qualities were real attributes of his personality is brought out time and again by the men, from different walks of life, from his undergraduate days through the war years, with whom he came into contact. It was indeed largely because of his tremendous enthusiasm that he led others to follow his personal vision.

Let me quote just one example of this power. The words are those of Walter Thompson, the Scotland Yard inspector responsible for guarding Winston Churchill. In 1921 Lawrence accompanied Churchill to Egypt. When they arrived they were met by a hostile crowd and it was soon apparent that the lives of Churchill and his companions were in danger. The crowd thronging round the Englishmen took no notice of Churchill as they menaced the small group. Then Lawrence stepped out.

No Pope of Rome ever had more command before his own worshippers in the Palazzo. And Colonel Lawrence raised his hand slowly, the first and second fingers lifted above the other two for silence and for blessing. He could have owned the earth. He did own it. Every man froze in respect, in a kind of New Testament adoration of shepherds for a master. It was quite weird and very comforting.[16]

And later he writes: 'Lawrence was so greatly loved and so fanatically respected that he could . have established his own empire from Alexandretta to the Indus. He knew this, too.'[17]

Then began the life of renunciation, but without reconciliation. Lawrence tried to change his identity, but succeeded only in altering the facade of his personality. In August 1922 he enlisted in the RAF as Aircraftsman Ross. One side of him wanted to escape from the heroic image he had helped to create and also wanted to work out his sense of sin through meaningful work. The other side needed companionship for he had a great desire to be among other men, to belong to some society.

We can see in his Birth Chart that gregarious nature, the outgoing side of almost all the factors in his Birth Chart, the Moon in Sagittarius, the Sun and Mercury in Leo and the Geminian Ascendant. Great as his self-reliance was he always felt particularly lost if he was cut off from his fellow men for any length of time. But with his inner sense of failure and distress, he was cut off from his companions. He wrote:

> From henceforward my way will lie with these fellows here, degrading myself ... in the hope that some day I will feel really degraded, be degraded, to their level. I long for people to look down on me and despise me, and I'm too shy to take the filthy steps which would publicly shame me, and put me in their contempt. I want to dirty myself outwardly, so that my person may properly reflect the dirtiness which it conceals ... and I shrink from dirtying the outside, while I've eaten, avidly eaten, every filthy morsel which chance threw in my way.[18]

He continued to sublimate his physical desires into his work, both in the exhilaration and power of speed in the cold control of machines – uniting his Moon in Sagittarius opposite Pluto with his Mars in Scorpio square Saturn. He taught himself to be an expert mechanic and was meticulous in his work and in caring for the eight very fine Brough Superiors that George Brough built for him, developing great technical knowledge and taking pains to master the technical details. In 1930 he began work testing experimental boats for the armed services and the Air Ministry gave him a free hand to design speedboats at Southampton.

He wrote at one point to his friend Robert Graves:

> You remember me writing to you when I first went into the R.A.F. that it was the nearest modern equivalent of going into a monastery in the Middle Ages. That was right in more than one sense. Being a mechanic cuts one off from all real communication with women. There are no women in the machines, in any machine. No woman, I believe, can understand a mechanic's happiness in serving his bits and pieces.[19]

Such was the answer of his Venus in Virgo to the primary influence of his mother through his Moon opposite Pluto and Neptune.

In February 1935 Lawrence, aged forty-six, finally had to leave the RAF. For a few weeks he wandered aimlessly. On 13 May he was riding his Brough to Bovington Camp. On the way back he swerved to avoid two children on bicycles, flew over the handlebars and suffered fatal head injuries.

Who was Lawrence? Lawrence himself, throughout his tortured life, was constantly driven to ask himself the question that in some way we all ask: 'Who am I?'. At the end of his troubled existence, was he any nearer the answer? It is difficult to gainsay his talents and his achievements both in the world and as a human being. He gave the Arabs their freedom, contributed in a major way to the War effort, gained one of the most brilliant degrees at Oxford, was elected a fellow of All Souls, wrote the *Seven Pillars of Wisdom* which Churchill regarded as the greatest work of any living author.

Yet throughout his life he suffered a continual crisis of identity.

'Who am I?' Chapman, Lawrence, Ross, Shaw? There in Figure 9.1 is Thomas Edward, great leader, brilliant child. Few have been driven to ask that question with greater vehemence. To few could the answer have been so elusive. Seeking his identity, searching for release, setting his mark upon his generation, on an alien people, creating a legend, waking up at night screaming with the recreations of his past.

We can see the conflicts in his Birth Chart, we can see the influences that created them. What theme is it that unites the different sides of his nature? Anthony Storr has described the psyche as a self-regulating process whose goal is the integrity of its being, contained in its innate wholeness. Lawrence, for all his greatness, for all his brilliance, for all the wonderful qualities that he expressed, never managed to attain that inner integrity that produces harmony within the psyche. As we look back at his life we can only be touched by the terrible feeling of sadness and suffering that filled his soul and that robbed him of the peace that he sought and that surely he deserved.

Lawrence could not accept himself. In spite of his achievements, and they were real achievements both in the world and in human terms, he was never able to accept his own authority. The reasons can be traced back to his parents – to the ineffective father and the powerful mother. But these influences are not in themselves uncommon and often it is these very influences which drive the individual to find himself.

We have seen the same theme in the other examples that we have looked at in this book. Charles Dickens never solved his ambivalent feelings for women that went back to his mother's influence and yet he contained both sides of his nature very effectively in his work. Gandhi achieved self-mastery and channelled his feminine side into his life's work. Even Henry II contained his conflicts in his actions and succeeded in uniting his realms empirically in the image of his own being.

It would be wrong to regard Lawrence as a failure. What is apparent is that in his own eyes he was a failure. No one succeeds

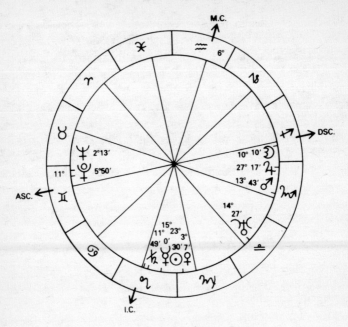

Figure 9.1   *Horoscope of T.E. Lawrence*

in any absolute sense and that is why the psyche's goal should be acceptance and containment of one's Self. Lawrence's failure, if he is to be regarded as a failure, is that he refused to accept anything less than perfection. The real sadness therefore lies in his inability to accept his own virtues and his own inevitable human failing as part of his nature as a whole.

We have seen that the conflict which is engendered in the psyche is produced by the ambivalence of the images that are created in the psyche. On the one hand the image, that originated outside usually from the parents, is transformed into an aspect of the individual's own being. On the other, with the inevitable negative associations that surround these images, the individual reacts against them. And so, in trying to fight what began as an outside influence, he ends up fighting himself.

It is only when he is drawn to face the images as part of his own nature by experiencing them and working through them that he can accept them, and then he must accept the paradoxes which are inherent in the conflicts. Then he can see that both sides, that which he has consciously accepted and that which he has fought against, are really two sides of the same unity and that each is an integral part of the other. Then, in containing and accepting the two sides he can bring about the state of harmony and wholeness that provides the integrity of his Self.

Lawrence had, from his mother's side, the Moon in Sagittarius and Venus in Virgo and also Jupiter in Scorpio as the maternal shadow. He reacted against the power, the sense of being devoured that is symbolized in the Pluto contact. He reacted too against the sense of deceit that is symbolized in the Neptune contact. And he reacted also on an unconscious level against the close physical bonding that was interwoven with sexual longing and repulsion which is symbolized in the Jupiter in Scorpio.

In trying to work through these conflicts he developed great power in himself with his Pluto on the Ascendant; he developed also great vision with Neptune close by, and he developed deep feelings with Jupiter's position. These, as we have seen, he sublimated into his life's endeavours but in refusing to face his real feelings he never integrated his feminine side into his being as a whole.

From his father's side, he had his Sun in Leo, his Saturn in the same Sign and Mars in Scorpio. In seeing his father as a hero, he developed his own heroic qualities but he was also afraid to accept these qualities. He sublimated the Mars energy, his assertiveness and physical sex drive as much as his female side and achieved great self-mastery. In themselves these qualities enabled him to achieve prodigious feats but these achievements were carried through at the terrible cost of repressing his own light, with the inherent danger of the repressed forces always trying to break through a chink in his armour.

It was not that self-mastery in itself was a negative reaction but rather that instead of leading towards his inner self, it led away from it. The results can be seen in the man who was driven always to hide from himself. Even his Arab dress was a form of disguise and his whole approach was self-defensive. Gandhi, on the other hand, in working, too, towards self-mastery, worked through his conflicts and so reached himself. The contrast is apparent when we compare the two men. Gandhi radiated a feeling of inner peace for he did not pretend to be anyone other than himself. There was a gentle humour which did not force itself on others. Lawrence, on the other hand, always had to prove himself. There was no sense of peace in his soul, of the inner harmony that breathed through Gandhi.

What was Lawrence's reaction to these images that moulded his nature? Why, with the other factors in his Birth Chart, did he adopt a Geminian Ascendant with the Pluto-Neptune conjunction close by and the other Angles flowing from it – the Aquarian Midheaven, the Sagittarian Descendant, the Leo I.C.? I have said that Lawrence was himself driven to ask the question, time and time again: 'Who am I?' How did he pose that question? This indeed is one of the most important clues to understanding his psyche.

Gemini questions. The way it questions is through the intellect. What is so remarkable about Lawrence was that, as a man of action, he should write a book which delved into his make-up and his conflicts in such a revealing, even though not a factual, manner. *Seven Pillars of Wisdom* must surely stand unique as a testament and self-analysis of a man's mind. But, in questioning through his mind, he also avoided facing the real conflicts which were in his feelings.

The problem is brought out in high relief with the Pluto-Neptune conjunction on his Ascendant. In that Pluto represents the root of power there is likely to be a question of identity in its position in the Horoscope. With Pluto on the Ascendant the crisis was that of personal identity. Here, literally, is 'Who am I?'

'Where is my power?'. His answer was to express his power in the world but here too he failed to find it within himself. With Neptune close by he felt the need for perfection, to assuage the sense of sin and deceit that dirtied him. Here instead of facing the void, he avoided facing himself and created a false image.

Lawrence also answered his parental-images with a childlike attitude to the world which is inherent in his Geminian Ascendant. His mother, dominating, threatening, so close that he saw her at least unconsciously as his partner with the Moon on the cusp of his Sagittarian Descendant, so close that any physical attraction to a woman would be like committing incest. His real power, contained in Leo with his Sun and its shadow, Saturn, is at the bottom of his Birth Chart. at the I.C., the roots of his personality where his problems began and ended.

Charles Dickens, too, was in many ways a child. Certainly the most original aspect of his writing is his angle – he saw people through the eyes of a child, from below looking up at them. But this too was his strength and he was also the archetypal father-figure in his own family affairs and in his image to the world. And the essential difference in Dickens's and Lawrence's child-like approach was that Dickens was that of the emotional child whereas Lawrence was cut off from his emotions.

Lawrence, in spite of his powers of leadership, in spite of his personal magnetism and the aura of greatness that he could conjure up, never lost his childlike qualities. While these qualities were in many ways endearing: he was curious, youthful, friendly and open with a sense of freshness that gave him boyish charm, nevertheless he also acted in a way which was essentially immature, like a persistent schoolboy who enjoyed teasing with his practical jokes.

Physically he was small, and the description 'insignificant' is often used of his appearance, his head being too large for his body and his boyish appearance never lost. Towards the end of his life Lady Pansy Lamb gave an account of meeting him at a dinner party: 'There was a crowd of people, amongst them a little bright-eyed man in a white sweater, who I thought was perhaps the local garage-man whom the Johns were befriending.'[20] Lawrence did not disillusion her.

This front was part of his defence, especially against women. Part of the quality was the anti-authoritarian side that resulted from his weak paternal-image. He would prick the bubbles of other people's pomposity, but like others who share this quality he was unusually sensitive to ridicule himself and he could not tolerate jokes made at his own expense. It made him stand up for the down-trodden against those in authority and to that extent it was a healthy trait shared by Gandhi among others.

But in Lawrence's case we feel it went too far. Not only did he reject the authority of others but he could not accept his own authority, his own inner being. With Saturn in the same Sign as his Sun, he rejected the Leo in others and in doing so failed to transform the Shadow into his own Self, and rejected both. Instead of transforming his Geminian Ascendant so that the Sun shone through it, we see sometimes the great Leo leader, and at other times the frightened child, and the alteration between the one and the other is unnatural.

There can be no release from one's own nature, from the factors symbolized in the Horoscope. Gandhi too suffered from his strong sexual urges, from his anger and irritation, and from his vanity. These he gradually faced and lived through. Lawrence tried to overcome his conflicts through will-power and self-mastery without facing his inner feelings emotionally through their experience. Then they were pushed under the surface waiting to erupt when something attracted them.

This is not to suggest that his kindness and humanity were unreal. Many have testified to his altruism and in many ways his life was saintly, as much I believe as that of Gandhi, and certainly far more so than Jung, for example. But Lawrence was trying to achieve something that was humanly impossible. If the incident at Der'a had not occurred he may have escaped to a monastery of sorts and faced the torments of his soul alone but even there he would not have attained the peace of mind, yet alone the integrity of spirit, that he yearned for.

In one sense Lawrence's greatness lay in being able to make his personal dream into a reality. To go out into the desert and unite the Arab peoples and lead them into Damascus was a tremendous achievement. In a sense all creative people try to make their dreams come true whether they be poets or artists or world leaders. Each in his own way is a visionary. Gandhi, with his vision, created a free India, Jung created a new way of understanding the human psyche and of healing it, Dickens created a new view of the world with his fiction.

What kind of dream was this dream of Lawrence? Why did he feel it failed? The dream that Lawrence held was an illusion. Not only was it based on a medieval ideal which never existed as a reality, but it was a dream that Lawrence tried to live out through others by projecting it onto the modern Arabs. Of his influence on the Arabs, Elie Kedourie was to write:

> He is a portent, a symbol of the power of chance over human affairs, and of the constant irruption into history of the uncontrollable force of a demonic will exerting itself to the limits of endurance. The consequences of his actions have touched numberless lives, and yet their motives were strictly personal, to be sought only in his intimate restlessness and private torment.[21]

Lawrence constantly sought to work out his dream through others; first through the Arabs, in a position that was in fact very lowly, a liason officer with intelligence and, after the war, through Churchill. If we look for the reasons in his Birth Chart, we see that he sought his identity with Pluto on the Ascendant. The power, *his* power, was contained within his own being, in his Sun in Leo, and to reach it he needed to face the Shadow of Saturn in the same Sign. In failing to do this, he projected it onto others and thus inevitably he felt that he had failed to find himself.

His need for perfection, his absolute standards and the resultant inflexible attitude which dogged him throughout his life, were summed up by him in 1934 when he wrote:

> One of the sorest things in life is to come to realise that one is just not good enough; better perhaps than some, than many, almost – but I do not care for relatives, for matching myself against my kind. There is an ideal standard somewhere and only that matters; and I cannot find it. Hence this aimlessness.[22]

The opposites flow into each other. The need for perfection, the Neptune yearning accompanied by Lawrence's utter refusal to allow any chink of love into his soul, his absolute refusal too to accept forgiveness. With Pluto on his Ascendant opposing his Moon he had the terror of being taken over if his defences, through his feelings, were breached. Lawrence, with his maternal-image, knew that if he admitted to his feelings he would be lost, taken over, smashed against the rocks. And the sheer terror held him back and yet kept him, during his life, at the brink's edge, hovering on the precipice, taking the risks physically, on his motor-bike and in Arabia, which he was unable to take emotionally.

Yet here is the need. The need to die in order to live again, to find himself through losing himself, to discover his real being at the bottom of the Birth Chart where the Sun and the Shadow lie – at the I.C. By refusing to die even a little, Lawrence ensured a living death, each day a new crucifixion for his torn body and soul. Thus he was, in the words of Ralph Ishan: 'a battlefield between purity and passion'.[23]

Lawrence was capable of great love for others but he was unable to accept other people's love or their acceptance on intimate terms. At the same time he craved their good opinion and exulted in their adoration. His shyness held a mask of indifference or flippancy which by its very friendliness prevented others either from breaking through his defences or of recognizing the tremendous needs he himself had. With his Geminian Ascendant and Pluto in close proximity this was his way of facing the world and others. But instead of allowing others to penetrate the shy, friendly approach he cut off his deeper feelings completely. As Woolley recalls:

> I do not remember him ever admitting to any affection
> for anybody though I knew perfectly well that in the case
> of certain people the affection was there and deeply felt;
> in all matters of the emotions he seemed to have a
> peculiar distrust of himself.[24]

Nor was his kindness in any way imposing. With his strong feminine side, he had tremendous empathy with others and a feeling of sincere love for those who did not threaten him. His brother Arnold wrote: 'He was one of the nicest, kindest and most exhilarating people I've known. He often appeared cheerful when he was unhappy.' And one of his service companions said: 'He was my only real friend, the only one I've ever had. He was one of the finest men who've ever trod the globe, better than Christ or any of them.'[25]

I have stressed throughout this book that in the outward differences, in the conflicts which divide the psyche, there is a unified theme. That, at the extremes, the opposite blend into each other. With Lawrence we have on the one hand his dominant maternal-image, tinged with deceit – the Moon in Sagittarius opposing Neptune-Pluto creating an apex in Venus in Virgo. On the other we have the heroic but false paternal-image that he was trying to emulate through his Sun in Leo square Jupiter and the consequent inhibition of his assertive energy in Mars in Scorpio square Saturn.

In feeling that he could not give in to his mother, Lawrence shut himself off from his own feelings. True, he sublimated them. He enjoyed companionship with his Moon in Sagittarius and he developed his visionary qualities and his magnetic power which culminated in his quest for the ideal in his work for the Arabs. In sublimating this maternal-image, and in sublimating his feelings, his Venus in Virgo, through Christ-like service, he achieved greatness. Few visionaries have achieved the practical attainments that were his and his work in Arabia was on any account a great achievement, as was his work for the war effort.

But, and here is the great tragedy of his life, in living out his dream, he ended with a nightmare. Literally breaking out in the night screaming with pain, terror and humiliation, and metaphorically with the blighted verdict that he was a failure, a fallen angel who had failed to live up to his ideal. Mack, as a qualified psychiatrist, has summed up his view of the man: 'His central, his unique, achievement derives from an effort to perfect the self, a shaping of his personality into an instrument of accomplishment, example and change. He sought *new possibilities* for the self.'[26]

To an extent this may be true. But I think the real point is missed in this assessment. It was not '*the* self' as an abstract entity that Lawrence could, and was driven to, work on. It was *his* self, and I think the lesson of this life is that not all the will-power, not all the self-control, not all the vision, nor even the altruistic love and kindness for others, can succeed if the individual tries to develop a self which is not his own.

Lawrence was a great man. But he failed ultimately as a man because he could not accept himself as a man, and moreover he could not accept himself as the man he was. He created a dream but a dream which dissolved because it did not reflect his own self whereas the true artist creates the world into the image of his dream because the world then reflects his real self. In refusing to accept his own feelings, his Moon image, he effectively shut out his own inner being, his Sun image, for the two are two sides of the same image. It was *his* power, *his* authority, which he could not accept because he could not admit his feelings and his authority and it was for that reason that he sought to live out his dreams in a surrogate manner through the Arabs and through the whole unreal mythos of a medieval world of make-believe.

His very strength was his weakness. His tremendous ability for self-control, the Pluto image that he cast upon his Persona, repressed his real inner self and blocked out his Sun. And, paradoxically, his weakness was his refusal to accept his real strength, to love himself and to open himself to the love that he gave so unstintingly to others.

Gandhi, on the other hand, with his weak paternal-image, his Sun in Libra unaspected in the 12th House, also used the self-mastery that Lawrence was to use so well. But Gandhi accepted his Sun's position. He accepted confinement and compromise. He went to prison willingly – his ashram was in physical terms a cell – he accepted his physical insignificance and joked about it. Lawrence, in striving with much the same self-mastery, ended up in the opposite direction. He effectively ended up a prisoner. But unlike Gandhi he was not a prisoner by choice. He was a prisoner in spite of himself because he could not face the shadow of Saturn in Leo, he could not face his own greatness nor accept it.

Afraid to lose himself, mastering himself, he was cut off from his Self. Gandhi mastered himself and in renouncing the outer values he found his inner self. Jung, though far from perfect, found his inner self and his own authority through the pain and torment of his breakdown. St Francis, who also dedicated his life to be a perfect instrument, lived through his passions and the temptations of the flesh. Lawrence, in trying to embrace the ideal, failed to accept his humanity wherein lay his spirit and his Self.

CHAPTER 10
The road to Emmaus – the potential of Astrotherapy for the future

Each mortal thing does one thing and the same:
Deals out that being indoors each one dwells;
Selves – goes itself; *myself* it speaks and spells,
Crying *What I do is me: for that I came.*

I say more: the just man justices;
Keeps grace: that keeps all his goings graces;
Acts in God's eye what in God's eye he is –
Christ.

GERARD MANLEY HOPKINS

I began this book by saying that man's greatest need is to find his spirit, to find out who *he* is. Astrology, in human terms, provides the means to see the individual. Astrology, as therapy, enables us to become the individuals we are. The realization of our individuality, of our own spirit, is, I believe, the real imperative of this age. That principle applies as much to those whose problems centre on specific mental disease, emotional breakdown or a more general search for self-understanding.

The Horoscope is the quest, the driving force that impells man towards the realization of his Self, that spurs him towards his spirit. Freud believed, in accordance with his materialistic viewpoint, that the goal of the psyche is the avoidance of conflict in the search for freedom from pain and striving, and that once the psyche is unblocked from the negative conflicts which exist in the unconscious, the normal process of self-regulation will take over. In this way the troubled psyche attains peace. Looked at visually we can see this direction pointing down, not only towards the earth but towards a gradual state of anabolism. And indeed Freud believed that man's aim was to find the path of least resistance for the discharge of tension.

To the Jungian this view appears to be a negative one for Jung's belief lay in the innate urge of the psyche toward spiritual realization and thus visually ascending rather than descending, towards a higher consciousness until we are finally united with the godhead. Looking at the situation in a two-dimensional way it certainly appears that there are two opposing directions. Yet I believe this brings out my point that astrology is really a way of perceiving. If we look at the reality in the 5th dimension we see that both directions point to the same place, to the centre if we like, and thus the opposites are united.

Freeing the psyche from its conflicts in the Freudian sense enables the individual to realize his Self, it enables him to form satisfactory relationships, to be happy with other people because there is no need for him to project his own inner conflicts onto the world outside. Thus the individual, happy within himself, will find himself and he will be able to establish effective relationships with the opposite sex and with the rest of the world. In this sense he will have no need, and no incentive, to strive for a 'spiritual' meaning in life.

Jung, from his esoteric viewpoint, recognized a wider need for meaning and purpose so that people could fulfil themselves and heal the sense of alienation that exists within them. Union for him meant union with the anima or animus, the female or male side within the individual. Then, when the individual had found union within himself, he could realize his creative potentials and be united with the universe as part of a greater whole.

It is not a question of which way is right and which is wrong, but of recognizing that both lead to the same place. The man who is happy with his wife and who has solved his emotional conflicts through relationships has found his integrity as surely as the man who finds it through creative endeavour or spiritual solace. Both have found their essence, their integrity, their spirit. The former is no less a saint in the eyes of God than the 'spiritual' person nor does he contribute less to the peace and harmony of the world. As Thomas à Kempis so appositely stated: 'A humble countryman who serves God is more pleasing to Him than a conceited intellectual who knows the courses of the stars, but neglects his own soul.'[1]

The need is for union. At the end there is only peace, the peace which the world cannot give but which every aspect of life strives towards, the 'rest' that Meister Eckhart described as the goal of all life. This, then, is the goal. The Horoscope used as therapy is the way. There is only one way we can attain that goal. That is *our* way. We can only fulfil our destiny by moving with the universe, in a continual state of metanoia, by aligning ourselves with our spirit so that we, being ourselves, are an integral part of our world and the universe as one living entity.

It may at first sight appear introspective and selfish to dwell on the needs of the individual and on inner change. But as Gandhi pointed out it is only ourselves that we can change. Changing within does not mean being unconcerned about others as Gandhi's own example clearly demonstrated. It means effecting an inner change so that instead of projecting our conflicts onto the world outside and harming those with whom we come into contact, our families, our neighbours and other nations, the inner peace that we attain is reflected onto the world. For, as Meister Eckhart said: 'If you love yourself, you love all men as yourself.'[2]

The potentials which are contained within each individual are symbolized by his Horoscope. Therein is that life's spirit. It is that alone which he can fulfil. The specific goal of the Humanist-Existential school, and in reality the general goal of all therapists, is to enable the individual to find and to fulfil his own Self. We are all surrounded by false images that stem originally from our parents and which can be seen graphically surrounding the factors in the Horoscope in the form of the diurnal circle representing the Persona. As these false images are introjected into the psyche the conflict that is life begins.

We cannot avoid these conflicts by pretending they do not exist. If we turn away from our own light, its shadow will rise up before us, darkening the world that we create. The paradox of life is that the more free we are within ourselves, the more in touch we are with our spirit, the more able we are to accept other people as individuals in their own right. Then, being whole, we learn to co-exist with the universe as a whole and with our fellow men and women. Then the inner light of our Sun shines through the wheel that circumscribes our lives and we radiate the world around us with our spirit.

The new consciousness that is symbolized at this time by the Aquarian Age enables us to realize our individuality. The corollary of greater individualism is the lack of security that has led to so much mental distress and breakdown and to the negative search for union by escaping from oneself through alcohol and drugs. The principle of balance is as true in the world as a whole as in the psyche. As the increasing technology of our new world dehumanizes its inhabitants, as the power of organizations becomes greater, so it becomes increasingly necessary for people to express their own individuality and in doing so to care for other individuals who are repressed, exploited and in need.

Many of the problems of this age are common ones. The stress and anxiety that drive people to drugs, alcohol or other forms of escapism, to marriage breakdowns, to acts of violence and despair. Whether the answer lies in finding a general sense of purpose, or of meaning in God, in work, in helping others, in art or in satisfactory relationships, it can only be *our* God, *our* work, *our* way of helping, *our* creativity and *our* relationships which we can experience. In the words of St Catherine of Genoa: 'My God is me, nor do I recognise any other me except my God himself.'

Therapy is concerned with healing the human psyche. Its goal is to enable people to experience their wholeness. The evolution of consciousness which we are poised to take now will enable us, through astrology, to perceive our wholeness. If we look into the future, as astrology enables us to do, we shall see the new science of Astrotherapy leading mankind to a greater awareness and experience of its individual destiny and goal in the universe. To accept our humanity and the humanity of every human being that forms this universe is the challenge of this Age. It is a challenge which must be faced within our hearts if we are to realise our spirit in the world.

Notes

Chapter 1 *What is Astrotherapy?*

1 C.G. Jung, *Freud and Psychoanalysis*, Collected Works, vol. 4, London, Routledge & Kegan Paul; New York, Bollingen-Pantheon, 1961, p. 339.

2 G. Szanto, *The Marriage of Heaven and Earth*, London, Routledge & Kegan Paul, 1985.

3 A. Storr, *The Integrity of the Personality*, Harmondsworth, Penguin Books, 1963, p. 168.

4 S. Bloch, *What is Psychotherapy?* Oxford, Oxford University Press, 1982, p. 1.

Chapter 2 *Psychotherapy*

1 S. Freud, *The Question of Lay Analysis*, (Standard Edition, 20), London, Hogarth Press, 1978.

2 A. Storr, *The Integrity of the Personality*, Harmondsworth, Penguin Books, 1963, p. 27.

3 ibid., p. 20.

4 S. Bloch, *What is Psychotherapy?* Oxford, Oxford University Press, 1982, p. 8.

5 ibid., p. 12.

6 C.G. Jung, *Memories, Dreams, Reflections*, London, Collins, 1963, p. 152.

7 C.G. Jung, *Collected Works*, vol. 13, London, Routledge & Kegan Paul, 1961, p. 14.

8 A. Storr, *Jung*, Glasgow, Collins, 1973, p. 19.

9 C.G. Jung, *Memories, Dreams, Reflections*, London, Collins, 1963, p. 153.

Chapter 3 *The astrology of eternity – the Kabbalah and the ideal Psyche*

1 C.G. Jung, *Memories, Dreams, Reflections*, London, Collins, 1963, p. 362.
2 M. Eckhart, *Sermons and Treatises*, vol. II, London, Watkins, 1981, p. 44.
3 ibid., p. 62.
4 T. Vaughn, *Anthroposophia Theomagica*, New York, University Books, 1937, p. 5.
5 M. Eckhart, op. cit., p. 55.
6 Thomas à Kempis, *The Imitation of Christ*, Harmondsworth, Penguin Books, 1952, p. 59.
7 Malachi 4:2.
8 E.C. Whitmont, *The Symbolic Quest*, Princeton, Princeton University Press, 1969, p. 294.

Chapter 4 *The Horoscope – the model of the individual Psyche*

1 M. Eckhart, *Sermons and Treatises*, vol. II, London, Watkins, 1981, p. 19.
2 A. Storr, *The Integrity of the Personality*, Harmondsworth, Penguin Books, 1963, p. 45.
3 A. Storr, *Jung*, Glasgow, Collins, 1973, p. 96.
4 E. Berne, *A Layman's Guide to Psychiatry and Psychoanalysis*, Harmondsworth, Penguin Books, 1947, p. 94.
5 E.C. Whitmont, *The Symbolic Quest*, Princeton, Princeton University Press, 1969, p. 194.
6 A. Storr, *Jung*, Glasgow, Collins, 1973, p. 48.
7 E.C. Whitmont, op. cit., p. 69.
8 ibid., p. 107.
9 J. Jacobi, *The Way of Individuation*, London, Hodder & Stoughton, 1965, p. 41.
10 ibid., p. 37.
11 ibid., p. 38.
12 E.C. Whitmont, op. cit., p. 165.
13 J. Jacobi, op. cit., p. 122.

14 E.C. Whitmont, op. cit., p. 191.
15 A. Storr, *Human Aggression*, Harmondsworth, Penguin Books, 1970, p. 82.
16 ibid., p. 148.
17 ibid., p. 79.
18 M. Eckhart, op. cit., p. 118.

Chapter 5 *From Ego to Self – integrating the Horoscope*
 1 M. Eckhart, *Sermons and Treatises*, vol. II, London, Watkins, 1981, p. 53.

Chapter 6 *All that is – time patterns of the Psyche*
 1 M. Eckhart, *Sermons and Treatises*, vol. II, London, Watkins, 1981, p. 37.
 2 J. Jacobi, *The Way of Individuation*, London, Hodder & Stoughton, 1965, p. 41.
 3 I use the term 'directions' here to include all predictive techniques, although I shall refer especially to secondary progressions and transits.
 4 By the term 'hard' aspect I am referring to the conjunction, square or opposition.
 5 M. Eckhart, op. cit., p. 253.
 6 Uranus opposes its natal position in Rosalind's Birth Chart on 20 January 1988.

Chapter 7 *Astrotherapy – the theory*
 1 C.G. Jung, *Memories, Dreams, Reflections*, London, Collins, 1963, p. 138.
 2 ibid., p. 145
 3 M. Eckhart, *Sermons and Treatises,* vol. II, London, Watkins, 1981, p. 318.

Chapter 8 *Self-realization – the process of discovery*
 1 E.C. Whitmont, *The Symbolic Quest*, Princeton, Princeton

University Press, 1969, p. 133.

2 M. Eckhart, *Sermons and Treatises*, vol. II, London, Watkins, 1981, p. 254.

3 A. Storr, *The Integrity of the Personality*, Harmondsworth, Penguin Books, 1963, p. 165.

4 E. Edinger, *Ego and Archetype*, Harmondsworth, Penguin Books, 1972, p. 168.

5 J. Jacobi, *The Way of Individuation*, London, Hodder & Stoughton, 1965, p. 134.

6 Quoted in L. Fischer, *The Life of Mahatma Gandhi*, London, Collins, 1982, p. 405.

Chapter 9 *A little lower than the angels – the paradox of T.E. Lawrence*

1 Letter from Lawrence to Edward Garnett, 27 August 1924.

2 Letter from Lawrence to Charlotte Shaw, 14 April 1927.

3 Letter from Lawrence to Mrs Hardy, 24 October 1930.

4 Letter from Lawrence to Charlotte Shaw, 18 August 1927.

5 Letter from Lawrence to Charlotte Shaw, 8 May 1928.

6 ibid.

7 ibid.

8 W.F. Stirling, 'Tales of Lawrence', *Cornhill Magazine*, 74 (1933), p. 497.

9 Letter from Lawrence to Eddie Marsh, 10 June 1927.

10 Letter from Lawrence to Foreign Office staff member.

11 Manuscript of *Seven Pillars of Wisdom*.

12 Manuscript of *Seven Pillars of Wisdom*, Bodleian Library, p. 445.

13 T.E. Lawrence, *Seven Pillars of Wisdom*, New York, Doubleday, 1935, p. 659.

14 J.E. Mack, *A Prince of Our Disorder, The Life of T.E. Lawrence*, London, Weidenfeld & Nicolson, 1976, p. 242. This excellent biography by a professional psychiatrist is of particular interest in understanding Lawrence's psychological make-up.

15 B.L. Hart, letter to the editor, *The Times Literary Supplement*, 3 November 1961, p. 789.

16 W.H. Thompson, *Assignment: Churchill*, New York, Farrar,

Straus & Young, 1955, p. 30.

17 ibid., p. 31.

18 Letter from Lawrence to Charlotte Shaw, 28 September 1925.

19 Letter from Lawrence to Robert Graves, 4 February 1935.

20 Quoted in J.E. Mack, op. cit., p. 446.

21 Elie Kedourie, *England and the Middle East*, London, Bowes & Bowes, 1956, p. 88.

22 Letter from Lawrence to Kennington, 6 August 1934.

23 Quoted in J.E. Mack, op. cit., p. 441.

24 A. Lawrence (ed.), *T.E. Lawrence by His Friends*, London, Cape, 1937, p. 92.

25 Quoted in J.E. Mack, op. cit., p. 442.

26 ibid., p. 454.

Chapter 10 *The road to Emmaus – the potential of Astrotherapy for the future*

1 T. à Kempis, *The Imitation of Christ*, Harmondsworth, Penguin Books, 1952, p. 28.

2 M. Eckhart, *Sermons and Treatises*, vol. II, London, Watkins, 1981, p. 84.

Index